THE TAO OF INTEGRITY

Legal, Ethical, and Professional Issues in Psychology

Barbara Lipinski

THE TAO OF INTEGRITY

Legal, Ethical, and Professional Issues in Psychology

Barbara Lipinski

Pacific Meridian

First printing, September, 2001
Second printing, June, 2002

Several sections previously published within: In the Best Interest of the Patient: Ethical and Legal Issues in the Practice of Psychotherapy.

Published by
Pacific Meridian
San Buenaventura, CA 93002-2808
Landover, Maryland, USA 20785

Library of Congress Card Catalog Number 2001116336

The Tao of integrity: Legal, ethical, and professional issues in psychology / Barbara Lipinski.
Includes bibliographic references and index.

1. Psychologists-Professional ethics. 2. Psychotherapy-Ethics.
3. Counselors-Professional ethics.
I. Lipinski, Barbara. II. Title.

ISBN Number 1-928702-03-1

Printed in the United States of America

To the memory of Alicja, Janek, and Stefan,

To the survivors and victims of the Holocaust, and

To all who engage in the struggle for integrity

ACKNOWLEDGMENTS

I wish to acknowledge the persons who have made important contributions to this work. I am deeply indebted to the graduate students throughout my career who have generously guided my thinking through critical inquiry. Your creative energies, enthusiastic feedback, and passion for dialogue and learning about practice parameters such as doing no harm, have sustained me. I have also learned about the practice of integrity through our work together.

I remain grateful to my teachers who have challenged, supported, and enlightened me. I thank Pema Chodron for the guidance in times of suffering and no escape; Thich Nhat Hanh for enlarging views on compassion; Alan Clements for silent retreats in Vipassana insight meditation; Bob Sauter, LCSW, for modeling a style of ethical decision making that serves as a framework for my personal style; Dr. Merna McMillan who exhibited grace and clarity during her complex decisions at Santa Barbara Mental Health Administration; The Honorable Yale Coggan for demonstrating immense caring during his legal decisions at habeus corpus hearings for the mentally ill; Dr. Betty Walker for existential insights; Dr. Frank Fox for consistent trust and vision; Dr. Rod Goodyear for support of my supervision research; Dr. Bill Michaelson for sharing the joys of empirical research; Dr. Phil Snyder for a genuine love of life, Dr. Adrienne Davis for exquisite forensic perspectives, and Dick Leslie, JD, for expert legal advisement.

My friends at the University of Southern California provided years of joy and delight through fruitful struggles, illuminating discussions, and heartfelt debates. I thank Dr. Wanda von Kleist, Dr. David Pope, Dr. Lou Sowers, Dr. Jeffrey Young, Dr. Mary Maresh, Dr. Shannae Rickards, and Dr. Jody Trager.

Colleagues at the Los Angeles Police Department have contributed to the foundation of this work. I thank Dr. Regina Chace for modeling a life of integrity and Dr. Azadeh Familii for valuable insights, guidance, and continuing support. I cherish our time working together in the downtown Chinatown district.

I remain grateful to Pacifica Graduate Institute and Antioch for opportunities to teach this material. A supportive community has sustained me including Dr. Mary Watkins who for her gentle, compassionate, and soulful manner in addressing issues of conflict; Diane Huerta, a lovingly respectful and consummate professional offering a welcoming presence to all on the Pacifica campus; Nina Falls, for heartfelt encouragement and great sense of humor; and Eithne Jackman for her unwavering support, open generosity, and kindred love of animals.

I am grateful to all those I have had the privilege to know through stories of their struggles as therapists, patients, and students. This text was initiated by these experiences. And I thank the readers of this book for journeying with me during the many months of reflection and writing. I have appreciated your companionship along the way and am grateful for the opportunity to share this work.

TABLE OF CONTENTS

PART I

The Tao

FOUNDATIONS OF INTEGRITY

ONE

water

The Tao of Integrity

The watercourse way is a path within Taoist thought "in which one flows, like water, over and under and through every obstacle, with a yielding softness that even wears away rock, on the way to the ultimate destination" (Singer, 1994, p.418). Taoist insights speak to the nature of an attitude that is applicable to the practice of ethics within psychology. The virtues of courage, wisdom, and humanity are suitable qualities in a practice devoted to helping others and serving society through processes of change and transformation. The five elements or qualities of the universe are integrated within this text: Water, Wood, Fire, Earth, and Metal. Water has been equated with yin or feminine energy and is associated with compassion, thus this work appropriately begins with water consciousness and ends with fire, yang or masculine energy, symbolizing a new view or awareness.

Ancient Traditions

Ancient Taoist traditions began before 500 BCE in China. The philosophical guidance provides a path or *way* to harmony with the environment, with other persons within community or society, and within oneself. The Tao has been interpreted as The Way and has served as the foundation for Tai Chi, a martial art that integrates movement, meditative practices, and imaginal elements.

Carl Jung (1973) admired Taoist philosophy and believed it exhibited universal principles that touched on "underlying truth" (p.560). In *Psychological Types* he relayed the meaning of Tao as the "way, method, principle, natural force or life force, the regulated processes of nature, the idea of the world, the prime cause of all phenomena, the right, the good, the moral order" (Jung, 1971, p.214). This "soul force" (p.215) or energy was also seen as a highly dynamic and creative process. The concepts and abstractions may be somewhat elusive to grasp since they point to a territory in a way that a map provides a sense of the landscape.

The *Tao Te Ching* is a significant and sacred text within Taoism, written by the sage Lao Tzu. The *Tao Te Ching* grew from *The I Ching*'s wisdom, *The Book of Changes*. Many translations and interpretations of the *Tao Te Ching* exist including the view of *Te* as sincerity (Wilhelm, 1977), virtue (Hansen, 1991), intelligence (Bahm, 1958), or integrity (Mair, 1990). Thus the path of sincerity, method of virtue, way of intelligence, or the principle of integrity.

This path moves beyond preconceptions and dualistic thinking, providing many interdependent possibilities between the poles of opposites such as yin–yang, evil–good, and black–white. This is quite similar to Jung's evolved thought process around the "tension and the nature of the opposites" (1963, p.495) and their synthesis. In *Mysterium Coniunctionis* he described a waterfall as the dynamic mediator or third element between what was above and below. The waterfall unites the opposing elements and mediates between them. In this manner Taoism attends to the whole aspect rather than one part, uniting what is separated and bringing a harmonious balance to life.

The Tao

The Tao is noted by two characters or pictographs. The three lines to the upper left of the Chinese symbol represent the incre-

mental process involved, progressing one step at a time. The lower left signifies standing firmly still. Taken together they represent fluidity and dynamism paired with a fixed, constant, or static foundation. Two seemingly contradictory and paradoxical aspects that suggest the nature of change and movement. These are the elements of the earth or visible aspects of nature. We are invited by this symbolism to ponder more deeply. ".I do not point the meaning, the symbol gives it; but what it gives is something for thought, something to think about" (Ricoeur, 1978, p.37).

The vertical lines to the upper right of the symbol crown the head below, representing the invisible or heavenly nature. This has also been interpreted as the source or beginning. The entire picture integrates aspects such as dynamic–static, heaven–earth, masculine–feminine, calm–still, and visible–invisible. The felt sense of the pictograph is broadening.

A more familiar representation of wholeness or integrity is the yin–yang symbolism which shows the masculine within the feminine and the feminine within the masculine. Another interpretation is being within doing and doing within being. The yin–yang symbol below is surrounded by eight trigrams creating a traditional diagram referred to as a Bagua (Lipinski, 2001a) arranged within a framework representing the world of *Later Heaven* or the complex world we are currently residing in.

Bagua with Yin–Yang and Eight Trigrams
Later Heaven

The Bagua theory seeks to explain the nature of the universe and the relationships between the energies therein. Each trigram has its own symbolism, meaning, and effect. The lines within each trigram embody yang, indicated by the strong, persisting, or unyielding lines "—", and the female energy yin, designated by the yielding, supple, or open lines "– –." The lines are read from the bottom up.

Each trigram has corresponding elements, life situations, and actions, for example, Kan (the trigram at the clock position of 6 on the Bagua, see the following figure) is associated with flowing water, the symbol of the lake and rapid streams, life situations such as career, ancestral concerns, and energy to take risks.

The following provides a brief description of each trigram as one traverses in a clockwise direction **KAN** from Kan.

The next trigram Ken corresponds to the earth element, symbolized by enduring mountains, associated with knowledge and self-cultivation (Lipinski, 2001a), **KEN** and suggests time to examine one's situation or accomplishments in life.

Jen, the trigram in the clock position of 9, corresponds with wood, symbolized by thunder, involved with situations **JEN** centered on family and health, and acts through thunderous, dynamic, or disturbing energy, putting things in motion (Walker, 1986).

The next trigram Hsun also corresponds with wood but is **HSUN** symbolized by wind and a penetrating type of energy that enters from beneath, allowing for growth and movement (Eckert, 1996).

The trigram Li, at the 12 o'clock position, corresponds with the spirit of fire, symbolized by heat, associated **LI** with one's reputation or place in society, and encompasses an awareness of what is illuminated by the bright light.

Kuen, with three supple or yielding lines corresponds with and **KUEN** symbolizes the earth, nourishment, and energy to gather, harvest, or bring forth into the world.

The next trigram Dwei, at the 3 o'clock position, corresponds to the **DWEI** element metal, symbolized by the mists and vapors of the sea, and the breath (Eckert, 1996), hosting stimulating energy and inspiration.

The last trigram Chien also corresponds to metal but is symbolized by a connection to heaven, exuding **CHIEN** a persisting and enduring life energy or creative action. Karcher (1997) parallels Chien to the dynamic force of the dragon.

These linear trigrams are paired up and utilized as 64 hexagrams within the *I Ching, The Book of Changes*, considered the oldest divinatory oracle (Karcher, 1997). In this dynamically remarkable and communicative system each hexagram represents the interconnectedness between the outer and inner worlds, portrayed by upper and lower trigrams, signifying clusters or groupings of meaning. The I Ching continues to be relied upon as a profound resource, accompanying those on transformational journeys, shedding light on the meanings of painful or difficult life situations, and providing opportunities for discovering new ways of bringing about or living with change.

Classical Taoist Approaches

In order to move forward one must first touch back and consider the philosophical teachings that have sustained time and continue to inform ethical practice today. This text looks back to the philosophical traditions of classical Chinese Taoist approaches before the current era and integrates them with contemporary methods. The guiding discourse in these classical views was social, or based in humanity. This differs markedly from inherited European ethical perspectives which split the ego and self into divisions of the rational and the emotional. This approach highlighted reasoning and relied on individual personal beliefs or desires in the area of morality. The classical Chinese traditions view human action in a very different manner and do not individualize obligations. Tao is considered as the public or objective social guidance that is expressed within a part of the social system, which may be an individual, family, or group. The social guidance consists of ways, paths, or routes of virtue. The Tao becomes the Way or the source of all principles in life. Apparently there is some disagreement in the literature on this *way*, and it is difficult to place into the concrete language of our Western world. Different situations may also call for different ways or courses of action.

The Taoism of Zhuangzi proposed flexibility and tolerance while the Taoism of Lao Tze extolled inconstancy, spontaneity, and anticonventional ways (Hansen, 1990). The Taoism of Confucius espoused the importance of interpretive intuition also known as humanity, in forming behavior. Intuition was applied to interpret rituals or codes of social conduct in order to experience conventional morality and build human virtue (Fingarette, 1972). Mozi or Mohist Taoism highlighted the concept of utility in measuring *ways* and emphasized the advancement of benefit and the diminishment of harm toward others (Graham, 1978). This is considered a utilitarian method that emphasized benefit and diminishment of harm as universal constants. The Taoism of Mencius theorized innate guidance, also interpreted as heaven's guidance, which grew from birth into heartfelt conscience, moral behavior, and practical wisdom (Hansen, 1991). These qualities were viewed as reflections of humanity, mirroring the conventions of the societal environment.

The Tao also offers the complex principles of nonbeing, nondoing, and nonviolence. Nonbeing provides the foundation for being since it is the space in which it exists. It hosts being. Nonbeing can be understood as the container in which being lives. All aspects of being are interconnected and part of the whole, thus nonbeing does not privilege any one aspect or part of being. Nondoing refers to noninterference with naturally evolving events. Action is engaged in but is not forced and is in genuine harmony with the Way or other elements. Capra (1988) described this as waiting for the right moment to take action. Nondoing encompasses spontaneity and actions that are not artificial but natural (Chan, 1963). Spontaneity is an expression of order arising "from the unforced unfolding of that natural order" (Loy, 1999, p.89). Nonviolence is a manner of respecting and believing in the flow of life on multiple levels, without having mastery over others or things. Nonviolence also speaks to a welcoming and inviting manner that perceives the beauty and subtleties in existence. This attitude allows for a certain outward softness.

The variability within the forms of Taoist thought pronounces a certain fluidity, flexibility, and interpretation of moral and virtuous behavior within social relations alluding to "a way of liberation" (Watts, 1975). The views differ but align themselves in the sense that we all have a capacity for philosophical wisdom in tapping a spiritual, innate, or intuitive guidance in acquiring and exhibiting moral behavior in society. This is remarkably similar to Jung's conception of the Self. The Tao's philosophical wisdom may involve perceptiveness, intuitive ability, receptivity, discernment, thoughtfulness, prudence, deliberation, caution, diplomacy, prescience, and judiciousness.

This wisdom is not only for sages but for each one of us. In a letter to a professor of Chinese classics Jung commented on the importance of experiencing wisdom rather than teaching it: "wisdom cannot be taught by words. It is only possible by personal contact and by immediate experience" (1973, p.560).

The Role of Wisdom

Wisdom is a highly relevant concept that provides insight into the development of integrity. In Taoist thought it is a function of spiritual development and does not necessarily emerge from chronological age, for young persons have been known to possess wisdom (Loevinger, 1976). Wisdom has been defined as "expert knowledge" (Baltes & Smith, 1990, p.95) in life, with "exceptional insight into human development and life matters" (p.97) with overall good judgment in managing one's life.

Sternberg (1990) believed intuitive understanding was a characteristic of wisdom. He also identified wisdom as a constellation of qualities including maturity, the ability to acknowledge mistakes and learn from them, a high capacity for self-knowledge and self-awareness, concern for other individuals, a deep understanding of others, empathic ability, possession of listening skills, and an ability to reframe meanings. Clearly, these are extremely valuable qualities for the practice of psychology (Sexton & Whiston, 1986) and for discouraging dogmatic thinking that tends to be active within sexist, homophobic, and racist thought (Hanna, Bemak, & Chung, 1999).

This full participation in life, or "deep participation" as Skolimowski (1994) has imagined it, is similar to empathic identification, "an aspect of the meaning of participation, thus an aspect of the meaning of wholeness" (p.152). A joyful and rich involvement in community and one's own life with the capacity to be actively aware of affective processes, hold thoughts about thinking, or metacognitions (Pesut, 1990), and perceive multiple levels of meaning as in the dialectical thinking of the Tao, maintaining seemingly contradictory perspectives (Lorenz, 2000) or opposing views of thought (Tolman, 1983) within a given context. From this lens, wisdom animates and provides a way to move within different contexts with sensitivity and respect for varying meanings. An interesting historical note: the term philosopher is derived from the Greek terms *philos* and *sophia*, meaning loving wisdom or lover of wisdom. Wisdom originally referred to the figure Sophia, a female divinity in times of antiquity (Irwin, 1995).

Wisdom

Being "comfortable with ambiguity" (Sternberg, 1990, p.155) is a hallmark of wisdom. This specific characteristic is uniquely attributable to wisdom since intelligence has very little patience with ambiguity according to Sternberg (1986, 1990) and tends to focus on breadth and depth of understanding. This comfort with ambiguity lends itself to harmonious contradictions. Dialectical thought processes tend to heighten and expand rather than limit or reduce perception, analysis, and understanding. These are socially transformative and empowering qualities of liberation (Martin-Baro, 1994).

These characteristics are valued by many cultures and tend to transcend cultural boundaries (Hanna, Bemak, & Chung, 1999). They are also qualities that distinguish effective therapists (Hanna & Ottens, 1995). These expansive elements of human experience unfold to authentic meetings between human beings (Laing, 1968, 1982), deepening the interpersonal relatedness.

Cultivating wisdom and learning methods to develop this important quality have been recommended, including Vipassana insight meditation (Hanna, Giordano, Dupuy, & Puhukka, 1995) based on mindful awareness, existential-phenomenological techniques (Hanna, 1993) that explore one's being and transcendence of self, and adapted awareness techniques from Gestalt therapy (Hanna, Bemak, & Chung, 1999) focused on centering, contact, excitement, and polarity. Methods that increase awareness, empathy, and metacognitive skills such as dialectical thinking (Arlin, 1990) are all extremely valuable in the encouragement and cultivation of wisdom and integrity.

A Way to Integrity

An attitude of receptivity and reverence toward the entire range of ethical issues that emerge within the practice of psychology can yield a system of being that becomes generative in leading to wholeness. This attitude along with our innate, spiritual, or intuitive guidance becomes a way, a process, or a poiesis of integrity. Poiesis literally refers to *making*. The reverential attitude, innate or spiritual guidance, and a practice centered in receptivity becomes a way of integrity, a process of integrity, and a making of integrity.

Integrity has been defined in many ways including wholeness, virtue, fidelity, honor, honesty, and sincerity. R. D. Laing (1968) viewed wholeness as a quality to be recovered within psychotherapy: "to recover the wholeness of being human" (p.47) was proposed as the essence of the psychological work. In affirming the importance of integrity Grudin (1990) defined this construct as "psychological and ethical wholeness" (p.75) continuing over time, integrating the reality of an external situation with an expression of one's internal thoughts and desires. I find this complementary nature of the inner and outer realities integral to the development of ethically appropriate behavior and the process of decision making. For example, a formal ethical code of behavior may be construed as an external reality, engaged on an internal level by the practitioner of psychology. This involves a process requiring the therapist to be actively and experientially involved in an exploration, through what Jung (1971) proposed as the functions of consciousness: thinking, intuition, sensation, and feeling. This dialectic of integrity differs from a blind acceptance and adherence to a set of codified rules. The perspective is complementary to Mohist Taoism which first examines the utility of societal codes and the benefit and harm arising from their application, rather than asserting a strict obedience to them.

The term ethics is derived from the Greek ethos, referring to custom, character, and disposition. "The root of the word ethics relates the individual to the group as a reflexive action, turning or bending the subject back on social identity" (Karcher, 1999, p.11).

Virtue and principle ethics (Jordan & Meara, 1990) are integrated within this text as well. Principle ethics are approaches that "emphasize the use of rational, objective, universal and impartial principles in the ethical analysis of dilemmas" (p.107) and virtue based ethical systems (MacIntyre, 1981) refer to one's character development. Principle ethics have been relied upon extensively in the field of psychology (Kitchener, 1984) but they are clearly insufficient as a sole source of decision making.

Clinical and empirical explorations have examined the qualities necessary for successful therapists. Personal, transpersonal, and transcendent qualities have been emphasized over skills by some. Whitmont (1978) proposed that the personhood, the nature of the therapist's interactions and non-interactions "and what fields, what archetypes, spirits, demons, or ghosts are called forth" (p.297) in the encounters with patients, were more important than professional skills or beliefs. Bugental (1978, 1990) has consistently emphasized the qualities of presence, accessibility, and expressiveness. Dass and Gorman (1985) emphasized the importance of being over doing in therapeutic work and equated the process of helping with the exploration and examination of oneself "at the deepest level we help through who we are" (p.227).

Organic Ethos

Ethics and the practice of psychology are undeniably woven together within this text. Imagine for a moment, a thriving oak tree obtaining its nourishment from the forest floor, a well composted soil hosting different organisms in the biomass, its roots reaching deeply into the earth, and its trunk, branches, and leaves exchanging the necessary nutrients with the air surrounding it. The tree exists within an entire ecosystem where energy flows in and out.

Akin to the noble oak tree, the fluent practice of psychology actively grows out of an ethical sphere, which itself grows and changes. The ethical structure is composed of professional codes of ethics, standards of practice, laws, and one's own character and moral development. Add to this a therapist's formative years of education, training, and experience within the field of psychotherapy, and the result is an organic ethos. A living professional field of aspirations and prohibitions, a diverse community engaged in active discussion and at times, agreement on practice and appropriate behavior.

With this intention the work on the following pages reflects an organic perspective, subject to ongoing consideration, revision, and further integration. Practicing with integrity is challenging and calls upon complex intellectual and emotional processes, reflections, consultation, decision making, and intuitive guidance. As Guggenbuhl-Craig stated "It is our sacred duty to investigate continually how a patient can be helped and how harm can be avoided" (1995, p.viii). These challenges and investigations are given a voice here.

Intended Audience

This text is written for individuals studying and practicing psychology and psychotherapy. It offers a unique perspective that actively integrates one's personal sense of wholeness with the application of ethical, community, and legal standards. Psychologists and psychotherapists are primarily trained in clinical, counseling, educational, or organizational psychology, and marriage and family therapy. They may be skilled in brief solution focused counseling methods, problem solving models, narrative approaches, and long term depth oriented psychotherapy or analysis. Irrespective of the approach, discipline, theoretical orientation, or training, each professional is required to function in an ethically appropriate and facilitative manner in their work with patients or clients. The information offered within this guidebook serves as a blueprint to a rewarding and deeply respectful practice of integrity.

Professional Resources

Resources are included to assist professionals who seek more information on child abuse, domestic violence, sexual assault, trauma, child custody, elder abuse, and dependent adult abuse. Ancillary information on professional associations and national clearinghouses for clinical and research information are listed as well as 24 hour hotlines or information lines for patient use.

For those intrigued with the forensic integration of law and mental health, information on child custody evaluations and the practice of mediation is offered. Crucial differences exist between therapeutic and forensic relationships, such as the rules governing privilege (Greenberg & Shuman, 1997). Thus psychologists or psychotherapists wishing to expand their practice should obtain rigorous training in these new areas of practice. Independent practitioners may utilize their professional skills in these forensic areas, which require a solid foundation in listening skills, an understanding of developmental issues and family dynamics, the ability to engage in critical analyses and assessments of complex situations, and a proficient grasp of ethical and legal standards. Both of these specialties welcome skilled professionals.

Terminology

Throughout this work, the term *patient* and *client* are used interchangeably. The historical derivations of the term patient refer to one who endures, tolerates, or bears suffering (Oxford Dictionary of English Etymology, 1966). This resonates closely with my view of the profound transformative process of psychotherapy. Jung (1954) described an endeavor of psychotherapy as assisting the patient to learn how to authentically bear suffering and to "acquire steadfastness and philosophic patience in face of suffering" (p.81). The term client denotes a function of the role, such as a customer, or "one for whom professional services are rendered" (Webster's II New Riverside University Dictionary, 1984, p.270). Given that patient is a term with medical connotations, the modern usage of the term client may be preferred by many psychologists. Feel free to use the term that expresses your perspective best.

Format

Part One, The Foundations of Integrity, addresses the foundational principles of integrity and practicing in the best interest of the patient, introduces the realm of ethical practice, presents decision making models and critical thinking, offers information on Protean standards of care, and encourages a tolerance for ambiguity.

Part Two, Walking in the Tracks of the Tiger, highlights the concepts of competence, including emotional, intellectual, and cultural competence in chapter four. Professional relationship parameters are addressed in chapter five with an emphasis on multiple relationships. A focus on the development of the psychologist is provided with information on the care of the self in chapter six.

Part Three, Centering the Dynamics of Practice, offers ethical and legal issues in the beginning and ending processes of psychotherapy. The basic parameters of confidentiality, privilege, record keeping, fees, and advertising are listed in chapter seven, while the closure or termination process and referrals are discussed in chapter eight.

Part Four, Crossing the River–Entering the Stream, begins with important issues related to abuse in chapter nine. Dependent adult abuse, elder abuse, and child abuse are covered. Responding to crises, intervening in suicide, and issues of dangerousness are contained in chapter ten. Additional forensic matters reviewed in chapter eleven range from child custody evaluations to testifying in court.

Prominent and highly referenced ethical and legal issues integral to the practice of psychotherapy are presented. Studying these will provide a foundational understanding of the ethical framework embodied within psychotherapeutic practice. Seasoned practitioners will find these issues merit revisiting, thus contributing to an ongoing integration process. The most salient characteristics of particular issues are highlighted within quick reference frames contained throughout the chapters.

This monograph contains a compendium of laws and ethical issues that affect therapists. While ethical codes remain somewhat constant and are periodically updated by professional associations, laws evolve more frequently. New legislative bills are continually introduced and laws are reinterpreted or clarified based on appellate or supreme court decisions. With this in mind, my intention has been to create an accurate and professionally relevant work, focusing on a selection of laws and ethical issues central to the practice of psychotherapy and psychology.

Practicing ethically requires a familiarity with the relevant laws affecting the practice of psychotherapy. For those practicing in California, informative laws can be found in the following codes:

- Business and Professions Code;
- Civil Code;
- Insurance Code;

- Health and Safety Code,
- Family Code,
- California Code of Regulations, Title 15 and 16,
- Welfare and Institutions Code, and
- Penal Code.

The following website is helpful for viewing the text of these codes:

<www.leginfo.ca.gov>

Please consult with an attorney familiar with case law and the practice of psychotherapy or psychology, when seeking the most accurate and up to date information on the legal parameters and if you are practicing in another state.

Ethical standards and aspirational goals are promulgated by professional associations such as the American Psychological Association, the American Association of Marriage and Family Therapists, American Counseling Association, and the California Association for Marriage and Family Therapists. Copies of these ethical standards are available from the websites of each association. The APA's code is undergoing revision and will likely be completed for publication in the year 2002. The ethical and legal guidelines will serve to assist in the attainment of acceptable standards of practice. Of course many psychotherapists and psychologists attempt to attain the highest standards in their work, and this volume will also support you in this endeavor.

Roots of an Ancient Tree in the Subtropical Rainforest
World Heritage Listed Lamington National Partk
Queensland, Australia

TWO

wood

The Realm of Ethical Practice

This chapter begins with wood. The element wood has been symbolized by dynamic or disturbing energy—with a penetrating type of energy that enters from beneath. Much is put into motion allowing for further growth. I believe a profound pleasure is waiting to be experienced in the realm of ethical practice. There are opportunities for immense personal growth when challenged with an ethical dilemma. For some therapists these experiences may be acutely painful, for others intriguing and perhaps thought provoking. At best the outcome is favorable to all parties concerned, at its worst, the outcome can be harmful to a patient's life and the therapist's livelihood.

My aim is to present the benefits of mindfully attending to ethical issues while keeping the patient's best interest at heart. A fundamental principle of ethical practice in psychotherapy is honored within this text, best summed up with the phrase in the best interest of the patient.

Lens of Integrity

How easily we lose sight of the best interest of the patient when struggling with the myriad of ethical and legal obligations that arise within psychotherapy or when relying solely on good intentions or the principles of self-protection and risk management. Holding our integrity and making decisions from a place of wholeness, allows us to consider the expansive possibilities and solutions. "The person of integrity is a continuous person, for whom the present is a point on a line drawn out of memory and into the willed future" (Grudin, 1988, p.51). A person of integrity will occasionally be "frustrated, embarrassed, and completely surprised" (p.51), and will learn from their mistakes.

As one begins to discern the complex responsibilities within a given case, a groundwork is helpful to establish. One reviews the central focus on acting in the best interest of the patient, including respecting autonomy, beneficence, nonmaleficence or doing no harm, and fairness, combined with accepting accountability for one's actions. Through this lens of integrity, one begins to view actions, responsibilities, and potential consequences in a new light. With integrity as a partner one proceeds consciously and openly reflecting on the parameters and alternatives in the situation. Revisiting written material on ethics, engaging in further research, consulting with a colleague, and becoming aware of any intuition or discomfort assists in the decision making process.

Consider the following scenario during an initial session. Martha tearfully describes her sorrow over the ending of her marriage, and relates her confusion around her husband's betrayal. She mentions how vulnerable and powerless she feels, as she did in her childhood. She's not even sure she can trust you. She reveals her ambivalence about taking any action in the ensuing divorce, but knows she must do something. She provides information about her husband, a psychotherapist, indicating he is involved sexually with a current patient. As she struggles to speak, you realize you met her husband at an ethics committee meeting last week. Near the end of the session, Martha wonders how she ever fell in love with her husband, who was her therapist just two years ago. You learn their sexual relationship began during therapy, and Martha originally sought treatment for issues related to incest. She prefers that you bill her husband for the psychotherapy.

The complexities slowly become apparent: issues of boundary violations, attachment, betrayal, confidentiality, and distrust emerge. Questions about competence to treat, informed consent and billing arrangements, scope of practice, potentials of danger to self or others, potential cross-cultural issues, and conflicts of interest arise. You are fully aware of ethical responsibilities to your patient, the foremost being confidentiality, and you are aware that no breach of confidentiality is permitted in this instance. You have a responsibility to provide the patient with the brochure Professional therapy never includes sex (California Department of Consumer Affairs, 1997) and you are required to discuss the contents. You'll need to conduct a thorough assessment and potentially consider issues of danger to self and others. You also plan to explore the extent of the potential conflict of interest in serving on an ethics committee with her husband.

One of the first considerations at hand is whether this is a case you may take or may need to refer to a more competent practitioner who does not have any conflicts of interest. If you can ethically take the case, what is your responsibility to inform your patient of your ethics committee involvement, especially in light of her situation and history? Do you decide to terminate your ethics committee involvement? Can you ethically bill her spouse for the treatment? What is your fee payment policy regarding who is responsible for the bill? How will these decisions impact the therapeutic process? What actions are in the best interest of the patient?

Occasionally, making decisions in the best interest or interests of your patient may include engaging in legally and ethically permitted or mandated breaches of confidentiality. At other times engaging in a legal mandate, such as a court order to reveal information at the risk of being charged with contempt of court, may be in opposition to an ethical standard, requiring a more complex process to discern the answer to the question, "Is this in the best interest of my patient?"

Therapists who are solely guided by their good intentions may commit egregious errors by transgressing boundaries and violating ethical principles, standards, and laws. Through my service on ethics committees, I have encountered individuals who articulate their own unique ethos, often believed to be a superior morality, eschewing the generally accepted group ethic or clear legal standard. For example, initiating a sexual relationship with a patient, or believing that physical touch and massage is a necessary calming component in a first session with an incest survivor, regardless of the literature contrary to the subject (Briere, 1989; Hunter & Struve, 1998; Pope & Bouhoutsos, 1986). Conversely, to be guided solely by the defensive posture of the risk management perspective, resulting in the attribution of negative intentions to patient behavior (believed to be driven by a litigious society), contributes to a fearful and protective stance within psychotherapy, limiting therapeutic effectiveness. An approach to ethics unifying an introspective stance with the continuous development of one's intellectual and emotional competence, added to an acknowledgment and assessment of the best interests of the patient provides a more balanced perspective.

Many are familiar with the Hippocratic oath initiated around 400 BCE. Considered the father of medical ethics, Hippocrates offered two precepts which are foundational in psychotherapeutic practice today: confidentiality and the obligation to do no harm to patients. The standard of maintaining confidentiality and the attitude of nonmaleficence (do no harm) are well integrated into ethical codes of conduct in the healing arts professions. These provide a solid grounding for working in the best interest of the patient. This text integrates these and other standards and aspirations found in the codes of professional associations, including the American Psychological Association and the California Association of Marriage and Family Therapists.

Awareness of Personality Characteristics

The Myers-Briggs Type Indicator (Myers & Briggs, 1976) is an assessment instrument widely used in organizational psychology to measure individual personality dispositions and preferences. The dispositions are assessed on continuums of extroversion-introversion (relating more to the external or internal world), sensation-intuition (how one takes information in), thinking-feeling (how one prefers to make choices and decisions), and judging-perceiving (utilizing a more evaluative or receptive framework). An individual is characterized as having one of the 16 personality types.

I emerge as an individual with the following type: INFP, or introverted, intuitive, feeling, and perceiving. These personality preferences, or ways of being in the world, are quite revealing, indicating strengths and weaknesses. For example, it is true that I enjoy being challenged, welcoming experiences that broaden my perceptions, allowing for more possibilities in life. I may initially reflect on an issue through an inner exploration noting the

Legal, Ethical, and Professional Issues in Psychology

nature and meaning of the experience or I engage in a journal writing process to become aware of my emotional and intuitive response. In terms of decision making, the possibilities can be endless when I think through a dilemma. For this reason, I challenge myself with the opinions of others, logically and systematically thinking through the details of the situation and discussing these, and evaluating the varying courses of action. Ultimately, the outcome of my action will be a combination of the exploratory processes I engaged in, and will reflect my personality style.

Awareness of my personality style assists me in acknowledging that I may prefer to work out issues in a particular manner, with personal reflection and a reliance on feelings and intuitive processes. This style could be seen as a personal limitation, thus in an ethical dilemma or conflictual situation, it is prudent to challenge myself by consulting with others in a collaborative manner. This provides a system of checks and balances in the reflective decision making process.

In addition to stylistic preferences, the process of making sound ethical decisions involves a number of steps, beginning with education. The training in ethics received in graduate school serves as a foundational base. But the educational process cannot end there. Ethical codes are updated and new laws are frequently introduced, requiring careful review and integration. Learning methods for analyzing complex ethical dilemmas may also be helpful. Unique or novel issues that are rarely encountered may require a new strategy for decision making, more information, or expert consultation. Education is usually the initial step, but in the best case scenarios, it would also serve as an active and ongoing process in one's career. Continuing education keeps us well informed of the guidelines for ethical and competent professional conduct. Not surprisingly, many state licensing boards have instituted new requirements for licensees pertaining to a review of legal and ethical issues. Many require a minimum of four hours of continuing education in legal and ethical issues for each licensing cycle.

Becoming Aware of An Ethical Problem

There are a number of excellent decision making models to employ when encountering an ethical dilemma. But how do you know there is an ethical dilemma? What is the process of making something that is relatively unknown, known? Even with the foundational education on ethics, we can encounter our personal blind spots, or have hidden biases, limitations, lack of knowledge, insight, or awareness about an issue. Professionals also differ substantially in the way they become aware of ethical dilemmas. As Gilligan's studies (1982) of moral development indicated, the very conception of ethical conduct, such as identification of rights and responsibilities, evolves from maturational experiences which are related to gender role. Although she postulated two disparate modes of experience she described a reality common to both men and women "the fact that in life you never see it all, that things unseen undergo change through time, that there is more than one path to gratification, and that the boundaries between self and other are less clear than they sometimes seem" (Gilligan, 1982, p.172). Her studies significantly broadened the literature on moral development and justice (Kohlberg, 1981) and the sequencing of moral decision making in the resolution of conflict in human relationships.

Given that we are likely unaware of some dilemmas, I recommend joining a professional association (see Appendix), becoming familiar with the monthly literature, reading journals, attending conferences or workshops, and seeking consultation and personal psychotherapy when faced with the inevitable anxiety that accompanies a transgression of integrity. Fortunately the unsettling experience of an ethical breach resulting in feelings of anxiety, may lead to the rediscovery of one's integrity (Beebe, 1995). At a minimum this practice enhances our perspective on professional issues and may assist us in becoming aware of an issue we might not otherwise be aware of. Of course, once aware of these unsettling anxious feelings, we can employ a heuristic research model (Moustakas, 1990) to investigate and discover the source. This

involves self-search, self-dialogue, and self-discovery, actively using our wisdom, insight, and intellectual flexibility to become aware
of the incongruencies. Employing the Taoist practice of nondoing
and waiting for the issue to become clear through mindful attention
to it from many levels may be an extremely helpful paradoxical
method. Regularly attending continuing education seminars on the
subtleties of ethical dilemmas and decision making is another helpful
intervention.

Becoming aware of ethical issues can lead to framing the right
question (Canter, Bennett, Jones, & Nagy, 1994). Asking the right
question can assist in a meaningful exploration of any potential
conflict of interest, assessments about level of competence, and
scope of training, education, or experience. For example, "Do I
have the necessary education and experience to treat this particular disorder?" or "Will providing psychotherapy to this patient present
a conflict of interest in any way," or "Am I altering my customary
ways of practice with this patient?" Clearly framing the right question is a developmental skill that is built on throughout one's professional career.

This brings to mind the internal supervision model proposed
by Casement (1991). Briefly, as we gain more experience, work
with varying supervisors, and consult with different professionals,
we develop inner personal supervisory models that assist us in
assessing and monitoring our professional behavior. From a self-
psychological perspective a revealing parallel concept to this experience is the process of transmuting internalization (Kohut, 1984),
or simply stated, integrating one's therapist, or in this case one's
supervisor, as a self-object. Thus an active and effective internal
supervisor is vital to our work, continually enhanced or modified
based on successive experiences, and may allow for the articula-
tion of the right questions. At times questions are more prevalent
than answers and open up many possibilities – asking the right
questions can lead to transformational experiences (Estes, 1992).
The traditional Socratic method relies on deeply authentic ques-

tions that attempt to understand the issues. "The art of questioning is the art of questioning ever further–i.e., the art of thinking. It is called dialectic because it is the art of conducting a real dialogue" (Gadamer, 1999, p.367).

There are various methods available to employ in the complex decision making process involved in potential ethical dilemmas. This next chapter presents several decision making models.

THREE

clarity

Clarity in Decision Making and Critical Thinking

This chapter begins with the Chinese character representing clarity. Becoming clear about an issue or reaching a resolution to a problem may entail an active process which begins in a murky or cloudy state. Efforts in critical thinking are essential in order to question, analyze, and make sense of the multiple aspects of ethical dilemmas. The term *critical* comes from the Greek *kritikos*, meaning to judge. Decision making involves a judgment process where issues are determined and prioritized. To *decide* is to "cut, to determine" (Oxford Dictionary of Etymology, 1966, p.248).

As noted in the previous chapter, personality style will influence the methods we use and the choices we make when faced with ethical issues. Let's assume that you have become aware of an ethical dilemma and wish to resolve it appropriately, with integrity, and in the best interest of your patient. Imagine the following:

After the third session of psychotherapy with Maury, a struggling young man who recently sought political asylum in the United States, you pick up messages from the answering service. An individual identifying himself as a close friend of your patient's wishes to pay for the psychotherapy and serve as a benefactor, but without Maury's knowledge. He mentions that he has already mailed a sizable check to serve as a retainer.

You are essentially an ethical person and desire to apply your standards of integrity in this situation. You are not motivated by the potential punishment or penalty for not acting appropriately, but aspire to a higher level of ethical behavior. Let's examine the potential problem first. An unknown third party has sent an advance payment for Maury's psychotherapy, and wishes that this fact remain hidden from Maury. We know that even the fact of a psychotherapeutic relationship is to be held in confidence. We also know that Maury is paying a minimal fee that was negotiated at the beginning of therapy. Perhaps we are uncovering a potential conflict here.

Participating in a magnification process is necessary. Let's apply Kitchener's (1984) critical-evaluative model to help find a direction for our ethical decision making. In this model, four moral principles are reviewed: 1) autonomy, 2) beneficence, 3) nonmaleficence, and 4) justice and fairness. We begin with autonomy, which indicates a patient has a right and the freedom to make his or her own informed decisions. Second, beneficence refers to the contribution towards growth and the general welfare of the patient and the active prevention of harm. Another way to imagine this is to think of promoting the welfare of a patient. Third, nonmaleficence refers to the maxim "do no harm" which calls on therapists to avoid harming patients and not engaging in risks to do so. And fourth, the principle of justice and fairness refers to the provision of equitable treatment for all patients.

With Maury's situation it seems clear that we would not promote self-determination if we made a decision on behalf of Maury and simply accepted the money, or did not share this information with him. In order to do so, Maury would need to be told of this phone call and make an informed decision. Second, how would we be promoting good on behalf of the patient, if we accepted the check or did not disclose this to him? We are now beginning to see that such an act lacks integrity and might prove harmful. Third, how is our possible action a potential risk for Maury? At what cost to the therapeutic relationship? Is this benefactor a friend? And fourth, we review this principle of justice and fairness, to see if we are affording equal treatment to Maury, as we would with any other patient.

Add a fifth principle, the best interest of the patient–is this action in the best interest of my patient? What decisions would be in his best interest? It is not in Maury's best interest to disrespect his autonomy, or to engage in dishonest behavior which has a potential for harm. This is similar to Welfel's (1998) emphasis on situating the analysis of a dilemma in the commitment to the virtues of the profession. Since the therapeutic contract is between Maury and yourself, you have decided to resolve this potential conflict by discussing the phone call with him and returning the check. As Gottlieb (1994) indicated ethical decision making and solid professional judgment reciprocally influence each other.

Another systematic ethical decision making model was proposed by Keith-Spiegel and Koocher (1985). This model involves sequential steps encompassing a description of the parameters of the situation, a definition of issues, consultation with guidelines, an evaluation of rights and responsibilities of the involved parties, brainstorming alternate decisions, citing the consequences of each decision, presenting evidence that consequences or benefits will occur, then making the decision. Developing alternatives and examining them carefully for both the potential benefits and consequences can provide quite a comprehensive picture of the impact on the patient and any other significant figures in the dilemma. Tymchuk (1986) developed a similar problem solving model, with a focus on the short-term and long-term consequences of the decision, and the psychological, social, and economic costs associated with the implementation of each alternative. This is referred to as a cost-benefit analysis.

Let us move on to a more complex situation, which we explore with another method. The following scenario unfolds at your new employment site: You are seeing patients during your first week at an outpatient clinic in the city you have just moved to. On Friday a patient referred by his employment assistance program, which has a contract with your clinic, anxiously describes a situation where he witnessed his next door neighbor's child being sexually abused two months ago in a condominium playlot while he was doing a welfare check of an elderly woman unrelated to this case. He acknowledged he was a mandated reporter, but had not made the report. You recognize the mandate to make a child sexual abuse report, but as a probationary employee, decide to review the procedure with your supervisor first. Your supervisor has left for the day, so you consult with the associate director, also a licensed psychologist, who instructs you not to make a report since the patient is well known and the publicity could hurt the clinic.

The feminist model for ethical decision making combines the traditional rational and evaluative models described earlier, with three other factors: recognition of the power differential that exists between the therapist and patient; the therapist's intuitive and emotional response; and the awareness of any cultural biases embedded within the decision making process (Hill, Glaser, &

Harden, 1995). This model integrates the social context of the issue.

With the above case, if one examines the issues from the rational evaluative and an intuitive emotional stance, a number of issues arise: clear mandate to report with reasonable suspicion, patient's trust and perhaps expectations of reporting in sharing this information with you (this can be explored directly with the patient); the administrative workplace aspect regarding the director's prohibition.

Your intuitive and emotional response may provide valuable information about the situation you are in including the political climate and ethical climate of the agency. And the best interest of the patient includes the clinical dynamics of this case: the patient has come forward, perhaps with a range of feelings about not reporting and is now seeking assistance in this matter. Exploring these issues, the options available to the patient, and your reporting responsibilities can result in an empowering decision for the patient.

An Integrative Model

I'd like to present the facts of a brief ethical dilemma followed by an integrative decision making model. The case (adapted from Pope & Vasquez, 1998) is presented here for you to examine the issues, reflect on your responses, and hopefully challenge your decision making process. Please imagine yourself as the treating clinician, including the empathic and caring relationship that has developed between you and the patient, then apply some of the steps of the integrative model to this dilemma.

During the fourth month of psychotherapy with an eighteen year old patient, you learn he has been diagnosed with an inoperable spinal tumor. In the next six months, he experiences numerous debilitating complications, two hospitalizations, and discovers he has Acquired Immunodeficiency Syndrome, AIDS. In a session he expresses an interest in becoming psychologically and spiritually prepared for his now imminent death. In the next few sessions he vividly describes where he would like to die and how he will obtain drugs to facilitate his death during those last days. He indicates he will discontinue therapy if you try to dissuade him from his plan.

The following integrative model is proposed for evaluating a dilemma and potential solutions in the patient's best interest. The acronym REFLECT assists in remembering these steps: rational aspects, exploration, feelings and intuitive responses, legal issues, ethical guidance, context of the dilemma, and treatment impact. The model is nonlinear allowing for a recycling through several steps, incorporates principles, virtues, relational elements, and contextual issues.

R E F L E C T

- Rational Aspects
- Exploration
- Feelings and Intuition
- Legal Issue, Rule, Standard
- Ethical Code
- Context
- Treatment

Rational Aspects

One begins the process noting the rational aspects of the potential dilemma, viewing the current facts of the matter in a logical and systematic fashion. Some suggested questions to ponder are offered:

- What are the facts in front of me?
- How can I define or articulate the dilemma?
- What is the patient's perception of the problem?
- What is the impact on the patient?
- What do I know about this case and what information is missing ?
- What else do I need to know in order to make an informed decision?
- What is the conflict I see or experience at this point?
- Who is involved in this conflict?

Exploration of Issues

The exploration phase moves on to an in depth exploration of the facts of the case. Begin to look at the issues from different perspectives, and think through various hypotheticals. Assess any distortions in perception.

- Evaluate competing views and become mindful of the opposing points of view.
- Write down support for each position.
- Evaluate the timeliness of a decision.
- If I suspend all judgments, what is the essence of this dilemma?
- Does this issue touch on any previous decisions or dilemmas? If so, describe this.
- What else do I need to know about this issue?
- Who might I speak to for clarification?

Feelings and Intuitive Responses

Any feelings or intuitive responses to the issues are noted. Contemplation, reflection, and the Taoist practice of nondoing are integrated at this level. Getting in touch with one's silence may be productive, revealing the heart of the issue.

- What is my intuitive response to this dilemma?
- How do my responses and actions inform me?
- What feelings or biases am I aware of?
- Do I have any hesitancies or reservations?
- What are my thoughts, feelings, and images about asking for help?

Legal Issue, Rule, and Standards

Next, the legal standards are reviewed. Look up the legal parameters or consult with an attorney familiar with this issue.

- Who is involved in this conflict?
- Is this a legal dilemma?
- Consult the legal standard for the legal issue.
- Consult an attorney, colleague, supervisor, therapist.
- What is the standard of practice for this particular issue in my context of practice?
- What are my duties and responsibilities as I now understand them?
- What are my reflections and responses to this dilemma at this point?

Ethical Guidelines

The Ethical Code and guidelines from one's professional association are reviewed.

- Is there an aspirational or ethical standard?
- Consult the ethics code.
- Identify the ethical principle or standard.

A helpful way to reflect on the legal and ethical aspects is to look at the particular facts once again. Whether the law or ethical code is clear or ambiguous in terms of the particular issues, we step back and evaluate our overall responses, adding another layer of exploration. At this juncture the decision making process may become more fruitful or more chaotic. Seeking consultation at this stage in the decision making process would provide clarity or a differing perspective of the dilemma. The efficacy of consultation from a colleague, supervisor, therapist, and/or an attorney is immeasurable.

Context of Issue and Treatment Impact

The context of the issue is also explored reviewing the precipitating factors of the dilemma, all the individuals affected by the dilemma and of course, the impact of this dilemma on the treatment process and the patient. An exploration of contextual variables are essential, including the similarities and differences between the patient's and therapist's values or characteristics, such as political views, sexual orientation, gender, class, culture, or religion.

- What is the context of this dilemma?
- Who is affected by this issue (including the patient's family, significant others, or friends)?
- What is the impact on the treatment process?
- If a breach of confidentiality must occur, how best to handle it?
- What is the impact on the patient of this dilemma or developing solution?
- Can I directly collaborate with the patient on this issue and the potential options?
- What is the patient's expressed wish?
- What contextual variables are present? Political views, sexual orientation, gender, class, culture, race, religion, developmental issues.

Solutions

This systematic process continues as possible solutions are generated. The same type of reflective process is employed for the solution to the dilemma with the addition of a criterion analysis. One weighs the options and examines the decisions in reference to the following criterion measure: Is the solution to this ethical or legal dilemma generalizable, proclamable, and equitable?

IS THE RESOLUTION
Generalizable
Proclamable,
Equitable?

Generalizable

♦ Would other psychotherapists in my position engage in the same behavior?

♦ Would this decision be reached by other reasonable psychotherapists?

Proclamable

♦ Is this resulting decision something I could confidently and openly share with my colleagues, knowing it was appropriate?

♦ Will it stand up to public scrutiny among my peers, professional community, and in the legal arena?

Equitable

♦ Is this decision just and fair and would it be <u>applied t</u>o <u>anyone else</u> regardless of his or her gender, religion, age, culture, ethnicity, race, language, sexual orientation, or economic class?

If the course of action does not result in an affirmative answer to each one of these questions, then an alternative course of action should be chosen. An ongoing reassessment of the dilemma and the effectiveness of the chosen response continues until the psychotherapist has arrived at the best possible solution for all parties.

Implementing an evocative exploration such as this will aid the therapist in arriving at the best possible solution to the ethical or legal dilemma. A significant framework of this decision making process involves a willingness to accept responsibility and the potential consequences of one's decision. Many ethical dilemmas are best revisited as situations change, "frequently ethical decisions have an evolving, unfolding quality" (Hill, Glaser, & Harden, 1995, p.35). These continued opportunities will allow for further exploration resulting in more effective professional practice and refinements in the complex process of decision making.

Standards of Care

Standards of care are duties imposed on psychotherapists. The acceptable standard of care is actually a minimum standard, not a "best" standard, or standard of perfection. A standard of care is formulated on a number dimensions, not one sufficiently comprehensive to solely guide professional responsibility.

1) Statutes, applicable state laws, and federal regulations, such as child and elder abuse reporting laws;

2)   Regulations of the specific licensing boards, such as advertising subtleties, supervision expectations, or training;

3)   Court cases, such as Tarasoff;

4)   Professional Association's Ethical Codes and Principles;

5)   Rules and regulations of the institution where one is employed (e.g., working within the armed forces would require knowledge of the different rules around confidentiality); and

6)   Consensus of the professional community.

The consensus of one's professional community is indispensable when contemplating an action that may be questionable. Framing a question such as "Is this act something I would willingly and openly share with my colleagues" or "How would my colleagues react to my decision to follow through with this course of action" or "Is this behavior endorsed within my community" could provide the necessary initial information for your decision making process, particularly if you believe your colleagues would disapprove or oppose your action. Naturally, the next step is to consult with other colleagues within your community, particularly those you believe would disagree with your course of action. Even in terms of ethics cases adjudicated in court, when there is no case law precedent, the standard of care applied to these legal matters is based on the behavior of what similar professionals would do in these instances (Hopkins & Anderson, 1985).

Based on this, the standard of care is at best protean, assuming different forms based on changes in the law, regulations, ethics, and common practice. A helpful way to remember this is to think of <u>Proteus</u>, an ancient sea god in Greek mythology who <u>had the power to change shapes</u>. He spoke oracularly, and would foretell the future, but only if he was physically held. At will he would change himself into a lion, a dragon, a panther, into water, fire, a tree, and so on. It was essential not to be intimidated by his metamorphoses, for then, and only then, would Proteus speak. It was a propitious moment when he revealed his vision.

Cultivating a Tolerance for Ambiguity

Contrary to other scientific disciplines, the practice of psychology, and more specifically psychotherapy, lies within the terrain of both art and science. The various theories of human behavior and change provide assistance in understanding psychopathology. It has been a common practice to situate oneself within a particular school of psychotherapy and its concomitant theoretical base. This allows one to be grounded within a specific frame of thought and theoretical explanation for human behavior. At best these types of theories serve to alleviate or defend against anxiety that inevitably arises when confronted with novel or ambiguous situations.

Alternatively, it is likely that there are several competing or complementary theoretical perspectives that one is faced with, or is actively integrating during the initial stages of learning psychotherapy, or throughout one's professional career. <u>It may be a more helpful practice to cultivate a tolerance for ambiguous or even competing information</u>. Another way of understanding this is to consciously confront and make peace with the anxiety that emerges when one does not know the right answer since this alleged right answer seldom exists. "Try to love the questions themselves" (Rilke, 1984, p.35) is perhaps a more appropriate framework for these issues. More realistically, gradients of good answers or responses exist on a continuum. Welcoming this framework of not knowing can open doors of possibilities, responses, and actions. This is clearly a fitting dimension of ethical decision making and encompasses the inherent wisdom within dialectical thinking and reasoning (Rychlak, 1976).

PART II

destiny

WALKING IN THE TRACKS
OF THE TIGER

FOUR

truth

Competence

Part Two begins with an acknowledgment of destiny, finding one's purpose or truth, and being open to what is yet to unfold. "Maybe the human task is to bring our behavior into line with its intention, to do right by it for its sake" (Hillman, 1996, p.260). Walking in the tracks of the tiger suggests an image of following something quite powerful, with a complementary attitude of respect and caution, for missteps on the path may have devastating outcomes.

Confronting truth is required when assessing one's competence, self-care capacities, and acknowledging the process of growing towards wholeness in one's professional work.

Cultural Competence

Pope and Brown (1996) conceptualized two types of competence: intellectual competence and emotional competence. Intellectual competence is the knowledge and experiential base, including the assessment, treatment, and intervention skills possessed by the therapist. This area is traditionally encompassed by scope of education, training, and experience. Emotional competence refers to "the psychotherapist's ability to emotionally contain and tolerate the clinical material that emerges in treatment" (Koocher & Keith-Spiegel, 1998, p.55), the ability to assess bias, and capacity to engage in self care. The threads of the Tao of Integrity are these competencies that form a full woven tapestry. Many of these threads represent a vital form of competence, cultural competence.

Cultural competence may be thought of as a category that spans both intellectual and emotional competence. It is essential to understand the complex role that human diversity plays in our work. Clinicians cannot remain culturally encapsulated (Wren, 1962) defining reality according to one set of cultural assumptions and failing to consider or excluding other viewpoints. This is particularly true given the culturally pluralistic country that has developed over the past century. The US Bureau of the Census projects that culturally and linguistically diverse groups will represent a majority of the population by the year 2050 (Sue, Bingham, Porche-Burke, & Vasquez, 1999).

The practice of psychology is slowly evolving to incorporate diverse cultural perspectives (Abreu & Atkinson, 2000). The elimination of cultural bias within the field will likely demand more time and intentional scholarly and clinical efforts aimed at broadening the theoretical base of psychology and psychotherapy. A focus on multicultural counseling, strategies promoting greater cultural awareness, and the inclusion of minority perspectives in psychology have been embraced by many who have acknowledged the Western European foundation of traditional theories of psychology (Atkinson, Morten, & Sue, 1993; Pedersen, 1994).

In one sense, all therapeutic interventions are cross-cultural, given that we each one of us differs in our cultural specificity. However, I believe <u>therapeutic work</u> demands that we become more <u>sensitive to variations</u> in being and more inclusive of multicultural <u>considerations.</u> The phenomenon of acculturation points to the subtle variations that emerge when individuals uniquely integrate or synthesize the values, customs, beliefs, and ideology of a new or dominant culture for purposes of survival. Perspectives on the environment, relationships with nature, and the significance of animals are often determined by one's cultural background. These values may incorporate harmonious ways of being with nature, a respectfulness of creatures, or champion acts of dominion or control. Through the process of acculturation, the cultural values may be challenged, broadened, refined, or synthesized. We bring these attitudes, values, behaviors, and historical backgrounds to our relationships including the psychotherapeutic relationship.

Sue (1995) described the goals of an ethical multicultural practice: 1) becoming aware of our own values, biases, and assumptions; 2) increasing awareness of the cultural values, biases, and assumptions of the patients we work with; and 3) developing culturally appropriate and relevant interventions. Awareness of and sensitivity to individual and group differences and a willingness to examine underlying assumptions, ethnocentric attitudes, and personal limitations, assists us in working with other perspectives in a non-judgmental manner and enhances our continual development and practice of appropriate, relevant, and sensitive interventions in working with diverse patients. When differences of age, gender, race, ethnicity, national origin, geographic region, religion, sexual orientation, disability, language, or socioeconomic status significantly affect our work concerning particular individuals or groups, ethically informed behavior dictates that we obtain the training, experience, consultation, or supervision necessary to ensure the competence of our services, or make appropriate referrals.

The Emic Perspective

The emic, or culturally specific perspective of groups, is a more congruent and appropriate way to work with diverse groups. *Emic* refers to culture-specific theories, concepts, and research methodologies, while *etic* refers to a culture-general or universal orientation. Emic approaches are helpful in understanding cultures through the eyes of the members of the culture. For example, several culturally specific interventions have been recommended to improve the relevancy and treatment outcome of programs for African American women (Roberts, Jackson, Carlton-Laney, 2000). These interventions include revising twelve step programs to incorporate positive and empowering statements for women, exposing women to historical and contemporary role models, utilizing affirming literature, and challenging counselors to shed the common stereotypes of African American women in order to break out of limiting thinking.

Cultural Factors To Consider

Newlon and Arciniega (1983) proposed a number of cultural factors to consider in the counseling or psychotherapeutic process: cultural identity, generational factors, cultural custom styles, language, geographical location and neighborhood, family constituency, religious traditions, and the manner in which individuality is viewed. This last aspect of individuality may be prioritized quite differently from the espoused American value of highly prizing one's individuality and freedom. It may reveal a more cooperative or collaborative sense of being within community, a responsibility to family over one's individual self, or a sense of personal value as measured by communal behavior, or personal behavior that serves or benefits the community or tribe. Individual values are often secondary to family in Native American, Asian American, African American, and Hispanic cultures (Gibbs & Huang, 1989; Sue, Ivey, & Pedersen, 1996).

Post Modern Thought and Reflexivity

Post modern thought lends insight to ways of thinking about and perceiving one's cultural biases and provides an interactive framework to understand projections. The process of reflexivity attempts "to locate the effects of the observer in the activity of observation" (Shulman, 1997, p.16). Cultural distinctions and differences are considered dialogical and socially constructed in this conscious, intentional, and evolving process. Dialogue allows for a critical analysis of the historical and social dimensions that contribute to the development of culture and provides a way to understand and negotiate differences. Multiple and contradictory realities can also exist within this framework revealing the true richness of this perspective.

Maintaining Sensitivity

Beyond a therapist's theoretical orientation within psychology, maintaining sensitivity to the variations of culture, race, and ethnicity is essential. Considering the patient's experience and felt impact of institutional racism, acts of oppression, and the influence of assumptions about social class may contribute another aspect of relevance to therapy. History of oppression (Locke, 1997), the importance of the kinship care network, historical trauma and sovereignty have been identified as important factors to consider when treating diverse groups (Korbin & Spilsbury, 1999). Although personal experiences of bias vary widely, the reality of racism persists in America. Failing to consider external factors when assessing and treating patients limits therapeutic effectiveness, impedes a positive outcome, and perpetuates oppression. Perspectives on relationships with nature and the value of animals, whether they be harmonious, control oriented, or of a conquering type of mentality are often determined by one's cultural background.

Guidelines Available For Assessment and Treatment

Paniagua (1998) provides guidelines for the assessment and treatment of African Americans, Hispanics, Asian Americans, and Native Americans. Sections present considerations for each cultural group and provide the cross-cultural skills necessary for avoiding bias as a therapist. Sue and Sue (1999) also offer important parameters in *Counseling the Culturally Different*. As an example, guidelines for working with Hispanic families were offered by Bean, Perry, and Bedell (2001). They recommend family therapy as the preferred modality and encourage therapists to assess for beliefs in folk medicine, serve as advocates for the family with other social service agencies, and seek to understand the sociopolitical oppression the family may have experienced by gathering information about the immigration experience. Holding a systems perspective is essential here.

Goals of Multicultural Practice

◆ Become aware of one's own values, biases, and assumptions

◆ Increase awareness of cultural values, biases, and assumptions of patients

◆ Develop culturally appropriate and relevant interventions

When Norms Are Not Applicable

Psychologists also attempt to identify situations in which particular interventions or assessment techniques or norms may not be applicable or may require adjustment in administration or interpretation because of factors such as gender, religion, age, culture, race, ethnicity, language, national origin, sexual orientation, disability, or socioeconomic status. When deciding to use tests, which tests to use, or how to interpret test results, caution is used when the patient is from a background significantly different from the normative samples. For example, the widely used MMPI, Minnesota Multiphasic Personality Inventory, did not include African Americans, Native Americans, Hispanics, or Asian Americans in the original normative sample. Fortunately it has been revised and the MMPI-2 incorporated a more representative sample. Many tests can yield misleading results if a person's group status is not considered. For instance, norm-referenced tests may lack validity when used with individuals from groups which were not adequately represented in the test's normative sample.

Scope of Practice

All psychotherapists are required to practice within a specifically defined scope, pursuant to the licensing law of the profession. Each state has a board or agency assigned with the protection of the public in the licensing of psychotherapists and psychologists. Marriage and family therapists are licensed by the California Board of Behavioral Sciences pursuant to the Business and Professions Code § 4980. Psychologists are licensed by the Board of Psychology pursuant to the Business and Professions Code § 2903.

Licensed Marriage and Family Therapists

Marriage and family therapists may practice psychotherapy and diagnose and treat mental disorders as long as the focus is on some aspect of resolving interpersonal issues, such as achieving more satisfying and productive relationships. This includes working with groups, families, couples, dyads of any configuration, and individuals.

According to one definition: "The applications of marriage, family, and child counseling principles and methods includes, but is not limited to, the use of applied psychotherapeutic techniques, to enable individuals to mature and grow within marriage and the family, and the provision of explanations and interpretations of the psychosexual and psychosocial aspects of relationships" (Business and Professions Code § 4980.02).

Testing Within Marriage and Family Therapy

Psychological testing may be used within the course of a marriage and family therapist's practice. Based on the California Attorney General's opinion (1984) on psychological testing, marriage and family therapists have the statutory authority to use psychological tests "within the course of their practice, within their field or fields of competence as established by education, training, and experience, and where such tests could and would be used to examine an interpersonal relationship between spouses or members of a family to help achieve a more adequate, satisfying and productive marriage and family adjustment."

Outside Scope of Practice-MFT

Practicing outside the scope of practice is a situation or focus of therapy not on some aspect of resolving relationship or interpersonal issues. Treating someone for smoking cessation, accepting referrals for conducting neuropsychological assessments, or doing a worker's compensation evaluation can be deemed to be outside the scope of practice for a Marriage and Family Therapist. However, the practical reality is that many issues impact the quality of interpersonal interactions with another and may be within the scope of practice. *Who* is in the room for psychotherapy is not the relevant question as Marriage and Family Therapists regularly work with individual patients within the scope of their practice.

Within Scope of Practice–Psychologist

The practice of psychology is defined broader than the practice of marriage and family therapy. The Business and Professions Code § 2903 states: "The practice of psychology is defined as rendering or offering to render for a fee to individuals, groups, organizations or the public any psychological service involving the application of psychological principles, methods, and procedures of understanding, prediction, and influencing behavior, such as the principles pertaining to learning, perception, motivation, emotions, and interpersonal relationships: and the methods and procedures of interviewing, counseling, psychotherapy, behavior modification, and hypnosis; and of constructing, administering, and interpreting tests of mental abilities, aptitudes, interests, attitudes, personality characteristics, emotions, and motivations."

Outside Scope of Practice–Psychologist

An example of working outside the scope of practice would be the prescription of medication for non-psychiatric diagnoses for psychologists who have limited privileges. Prescription privileges are currently not permitted in most jurisdictions, but a movement has begun to expand the privilege of prescribing psychiatric medication to psychologists who have received the requisite education and training. Successful provisional trials have already involved military psychologists with prescription privileges.

Scope of Training and/or Experience

Once it is determined the work is within the Scope of Practice the next filter is determining whether the professional has sufficient training and/or experience. If yes, then the treatment proceeds. If no, then the treating therapist needs to either secure the required training (through education, supervision, research, consultation, etc.) within a reasonable time period, or she or he needs to refer the case out for treatment of the issues involved. For example, a patient reports the symptoms of bulimia during the fourth session of treatment for relationship difficulties, and the treating therapist has a reasonable amount of training in eating disorders, but does not have a reasonable amount of experience in dealing with this specialized issue. Prudent behavior on the part of the therapist involves obtaining supervision or consultation. However, depending on the therapist's limitations, referring the case out to a more experienced psychotherapist may be necessary.

Professional and Unprofessional Conduct

Once licensed as a professional psychologist or psychotherapist, one is held accountable for a range of behaviors related to the qualification, functions, or duties of a licensee. In California, the Board of Psychology and the Board of Behavioral Sciences may deny, suspend, or revoke the privilege to practice. Some gross departures from acceptable standards of practice are presented along with other circumstances that constitute unprofessional conduct.

♦ Unprofessional conduct includes performing or holding oneself out as able to perform professional services beyond one's field or field of competence as established by education, training, and/or experience (Business & Professions Code § 4982). Misrepresenting the type or status of a license is also included here.

♦ Failing to comply with the child abuse reporting requirements of Penal Code § 11166.

♦ Conviction of a crime substantially related to the qualifications, functions, or duties of a licensee.

- Using any controlled substance or specified dangerous drug, or any alcoholic beverage to a dangerous or injurious extent, or to the extent that such use impairs one's ability to conduct responsibilities with safety to the public. Also, conviction of more than one misdemeanor or any felony involving the use, consumption, or self-administration of any referred to substance.

- Intentionally or recklessly causing physical or emotional harm to any patient.

- Commission of any dishonest, or fraudulent act substantially related to the qualifications, functions, or duties of a licensee.

- Engaging in sexual relations with a patient, soliciting sexual relationship with a patient, or committing an act of sexual abuse, or sexual misconduct with a patient, or committing an act punishable as a sexually related crime, if substantially related to the qualifications, functions, or duties of a marriage, family, and child counselor.

- Failure to maintain confidentiality, except as otherwise required or permitted by law, of all information that has been received from a patient in confidence during the course of treatment and all information about the patient which is obtained from tests or other means.

♦ Regarding informed consent and practice: prior to the commencement of treatment, failing to disclose to the patient or prospective patient the fee to be charged for the professional services, or the basis upon which that fee will be computed.

♦ Paying, accepting, or soliciting any consideration, compensation, or remuneration, for the referral of professional patients. However, fees for collaboration among two or more licensees in a case or cases are permitted when properly disclosed.

♦ Reproduction or description in public of any psychological test or other assessment device, the value of which depends in whole or in part on the naiveté of the subject in ways that might invalidate the test or device.

Values and Biases

Therapists carry their own values, beliefs, and biases into sessions, which impact their therapeutic decisions, and are likely to influence the direction and outcome of the therapy. Therefore, to the extent possible, it is extremely important that therapists:

Become aware of personal values and biases. Clarification of personal values is the first essential step; Determine how these values and attitudes affect or interfere with clinical practice; and discuss with patients those values that are part of the treatment approach, whenever appropriate. For example, when working with a couple, it is helpful to disclose your bias if you favor the couple staying together. Being clear and explicit about your bias will assist your patients. Having the courage and commitment to deeply examine one's values and beliefs is essential.

During the last several years, the consciousness of many professional communities has been raised in the direction of a more active form of psychotherapy, taking into account the individual's or family's ecological framework including the community lived in. Beginning to perceive the individual seated within the psychotherapeutic consulting room as more than one person with an internal psychic life, but an individual living within a context, a web of life interacting with friends, family, coworkers, peers, children, etc. Clinical training programs are increasingly integrating a family and societal perspective into coursework, and the focus expands beyond the individual.

Assisting an individual to become well, to find one's own voice, discover one's personal power, to learn new coping strategies, to be free of destructive relationships, and to heal from past trauma, are distinguishing characteristics of psychotherapy. And all of these aspects are best grounded within the social and cultural context each individual lives, works, and thrives in, keeping in mind the individual differences within and across cultural groups. Our responsibilities to become aware of the cultural contexts our patients exist in along with our own internalized societal attitudes and values are called for. Respecting and appreciating the differences, being comfortable with the differences, and having the ability to change any false beliefs we may hold are all necessary components in the process.

Illuminating the mysteries of one's idiosyncratic biases and ways of being in the world can be extremely empowering for the therapist, yielding a profound personal awareness that leads to an expansion of choices in ethical dilemmas and the continued development of integrity.

FIVE

honor

Professional Relationships

Many psychologists and psychotherapists describe a calling to this work, a true vocation. This may be extremely clear from the outset, may become apparent at a significant point in training, or is discovered through the resources or assistance of concerned others as noted by James Hillman in *The Soul's Code*

(1996). A calling may be resisted when heard or slowly revealed through various twists along the way. The calling frequently involves both being and doing and can have the felt sense of what Joseph Campbell once termed "following your bliss."

Whether you have heard and followed your calling, made a logical and rational career decision, or continue on a sojourn to discern the precise form of your future work, understanding the range of issues discussed in this chapter provides a foundation for the practice of psychotherapy. The practice of psychotherapy is centered in both privilege and responsibility (Edinger, 1997). We are responsible to our patients, ourselves, and the broader community. This chapter considers our professional relationships.

Multiple Relationships

Multiple relationships with patients occur when a psychotherapist "engages in another, significantly different relationship with the patient" (Pope, 1991, p. 21). Ethical problems often emerge when therapists expand their professional relationship with a patient into another kind of relationship. Of course, multiple relationships may be inevitable where it is not feasible to avoid social and nonprofessional contact, such as in small communities (Biaggio & Greene, 1995). Small communities may be designated by geography such as rural communities (Gates & Speare, 1990), or affiliation, as in ethnic minority communities (Sears, 1990) and gay or lesbian communities (Smith, 1990).

Overlapping Relationships

In fact, Berman (1990) developed the term overlapping relationships to describe the unavoidable types of multiple relationships that may occur for therapists and their patients. The American Psychological Association also acknowledged "In many communities and situations, it may not be feasible or reasonable for psychologists to avoid social or other nonprofessional contacts with persons such as patients, clients, students, supervisees, or research participants" (1992, p. 1601).

These overlapping types of relationships are considered to be problematic if they impair the therapist's objectivity or harm or exploit the patient. Fortunately, the Feminist Therapy Code of Ethics (Feminist Therapy Institute, 1987) provides guidelines regarding the management of overlapping relationships. The guidelines encourage the self-monitoring of one's public and private statements and strictly prohibits any sexual intimacies or overtly or covertly sexualized behaviors with a client or former client (Section IIIa,b,c). Discussing the possibilities of running into patients within small communities provides information on how to handle these situations in the patient's best interest. In most ethical codes, the therapist is responsible for maintaining professional boundaries, thus a therapist initiated discussion would provide an opportunity for the patient to disclose thoughts and feelings about these potential encounters prior to their occurrence.

Finding Oneself in Unexpected Situations

From an entirely different perspective, Arons and Siegel (1995) described the consequences of finding oneself in unexpected situations with patients, such as encountering a patient while engaging in religious or political activities, or at a nude beach, or in a queue for an x-rated film. They paralleled the therapist's experience to the exposure of the Wizard of Oz by Toto; being seen in one's full human vulnerability by a patient, the way the wizard was seen once the cloth curtain was pulled aside. They noted feelings of shame and inadequacy and concerns about losing patients. These feelings and concerns can affect the therapeutic relationship through the transference and countertransference. Preparing for these kinds of encounters through imaginal exercises or personal psychotherapy can provide "insight into which parts of our professional persona are there to support our work and which parts stem from our fears, self-criticism, and difficulty accepting unexamined aspects of ourselves" (p. 134). Self-exploration around these issues can benefit the psychotherapist as well as the patient.

Multiple relationship violations can result in license suspension or revocation actions and potential civil liability if sued by a patient. They are primarily an ethical rather than a legal prohibition, with the exception of sexual relationships, which are legal prohibitions.

Multiple Relationships

Psychotherapists must be cognizant of their potentially influential position with respect to patients, and they avoid exploiting trust and dependency, avoiding multiple relationships with patients that could impair their professional judgment or increase the risk of exploitation.

Multiple Relationships Generally Include:
1. Sexual relationships.
2. Bartering or trading for services.
   Although not prohibited, psychotherapists ordinarily refrain from bartering because such arrangements create inherent risks, potential for conflicts, exploitation, and distortion of the professional relationship. One may barter only if it is not clinically contraindicated, and the relationship is not exploitative.

3. Business or financial transactions outside the scope of the professional therapy relationship.
4. Supervisorial or teacher-student relationships.
5. Social relationships that interfere with the best interests of the patient.

Psychotherapist-Patient Sexual Intimacy

Any kind of sexual contact, asking for sexual exploitation, or sexual misconduct by a psychotherapist with a patient is categorized as illegal, unethical, and unprofessional. *Sexual contact* means touching an intimate part (sexual organ, anus, buttocks, groin, or breast) of another person. *Touching* means physical contact with another person either through the person's clothes or directly with the person's skin (e.g. intercourse, fondling, etc.). *Sexual misconduct* includes nudity, kissing, spanking, as well as sexual suggestions or innuendoes.

The above prohibitions are applicable both during the professional relationship, and for two years following termination of therapy.

The criminal offense is coupled with a penalty in many states. In California the first offense is a misdemeanor. Subsequent violations are treated either as misdemeanor or felony violations. Any proven offense also subjects the therapist to license suspension and/or revocation and civil liability.

Any psychotherapist who becomes aware that his/her patient had alleged sexual intercourse or sexual contact with a previous psychotherapist during the course of a prior treatment, provides the patient a brochure promulgated by the Department of Consumer Affairs which delineates the rights of and remedies for patients who have been sexually involved with their psychotherapist. Furthermore, the psychotherapist is required to discuss the contents with the patient. No breach of confidentiality is permitted in these instances.

Eros and the Experience of Countertransference

I believe it is not unusual to experience a deep prizing, love, or attraction toward a patient during the course of treatment. In fact this experience or the lack of it, can serve as a powerful assessment and therapeutic tool revealing a depth of clinical information not available in another form. Unfortunately this topic is often perceived as taboo, relegated to the shadow, perhaps among practitioners who have not received training or instruction in how to address these human emotions and experiences when they emerge during psychotherapy. On the contrary, this needs to be a topic that we seek to understand, openly discuss, willingly consult about, and examine mindfully.

Eros emerges within psychotherapy and may be present throughout the entire treatment process. In Greek mythology Eros the god brought individuals together within a community, was considered a god of attraction, and was honored for inspiring passion. Eros signified a sexual love in ancient times, in distinction to agape, an altruistic love, or philia, viewed as brotherly love or friendly affection. Jung (1960) broadened the modern understanding of eros by accurately interpreting this concept as life force energy and creative power. If viewed as creative power and life force energy that can also manifest sexually but does not do so exclusively, eros becomes less threatening or fear invoking. Indeed many therapists experience cognitive dissonance when faced with a discussion of eros and its misunderstood expression within the therapeutic setting. Eros and the experience of countertransference, or erotic countertransference, remains both a goldmine and minefield (Hedges, Hilton, Hilton, & Caudill, 1997).

An Animating Quality

The presence of eros, a creative power, vitality, and life force energy can be viewed as a foundational element within the psychotherapeutic process. Eros as a contributor to the archetypal field psychotherapy is contained in. Eros as an *animating* quality, a soulful force. This pertains to a form of human connection, engagement, love, an inspiring empathy, a passionate creativity, within this process. It resides in a liminal space between the individuals, within the intersubjective field, in the imaginal realm, in the therapeutic consulting room and serves a therapeutic purpose. But neither individual becomes identified with it, overpowered by it, or possessed by it. This speaks to a soulful resonance or interpersonal connection. Samuels' (1989) concept of *embodied countertransference* as the physical, actual, material, and sensual expression within the therapist of something in the patient's inner world seems to speak to this realm beautifully. Schwartz-Salant (1984) wrote on the *subtle body*, a phenomenon that exists outside the usual sense of time within the imaginal realm, that allows a flowing of attention through one's heart toward another person. These are generative qualities that invoke the presence of eros and not sexual enactments or transgressions of boundaries.

Awareness of One's Own Responses

Therapists are trained to assess and analyze the transference and may be more comfortable with this perspective in distinction to a focus on countertransference. Learning to tolerate transference responses such as strong attachments, dependency needs, and idealization are important skills. These attachments, needs, and idealizations may also generate countertransference reactions within the therapist that benefit from exploration. The capacity to become aware of and monitor responses serves our patients well.

Awareness of Patient's Experience

Maintaining sensitivity to the consequences from the earlier boundary violations experienced by the patient and respecting appropriate boundaries remains integral in the treatment process. Covert or overt sexualization of the relationship is not engaged in (American Psychological Association, 1992) and self-disclosure is used when it is in the best interest of the patient (Brown, 1991).

The manner of the self-disclosure, the context, and the benefit to the patient are all important elements (Guttheil & Gabbard, 1998).

Hayden (1996) astutely observed that a patient's erotic feelings may be only a small part of the entire range of intense feelings that are transference based. In noting the power struggles that may emerge within psychotherapy, she indicated the communication of sexual feelings always took place in a context of interpersonal power. Therapeutic work may restimulate earlier "confusions about how affection, dependency, vulnerability, sexuality and power are intertwined" (p.13). Thus, feelings of sexual arousal may exist for patients who are feeling heard or are experiencing a sense of deep connection. The sexual arousal may result in shame based or angry feelings. When patients are not able to tolerate these feelings, they can be projected onto the therapist who may experience great discomfort or projective identification. Mindfully discerning these countertransference reactions and sensitively processing and framing responses or interpreting the transference may lead to invaluable insights about prior abusive relational dynamics.

Eros As Sexual Attraction

In terms of eros as sexual attraction, studies indicate the phenomenon of sexual attraction to patients is statistically normal (Pope & Bouhoutsos, 1986) and "may be a completely natural part of the therapist's reaction to some patients" (p.36). However, acting on the sexual attraction and engaging in sexual enactments is not. Additionally sexual involvement is both ethically and legally prohibited, although these restrictions have not served to persuade some therapists against betraying the trust of their patients.

In place of allowing these issues to remain in the collective shadow, defending against, denying, fleeing from, or avoiding the emergence of eros within psychotherapy or the erotic nature of the work including sexual attraction, we can look mindfully, explore consciously, sensitively, and clearly at these complex feelings including the absence of them. This process of *seeing through* can lead to a profound understanding of the patient, the therapeutic process, and of ourselves. In this way we are relying on eros as a therapeutic resource.

Baur (1999) examined how the psychotherapy profession has responded to the intricacies and ambiguities of love in psychotherapy. She implied that we may be fearful about learning more about ourselves, or of being like our patients, thus exposing our vulnerability. Schamess (1999) encouraged therapists to recognize erotic content within therapy as "an important, but not necessarily central component of treatment" (p.26). This added dimension serves to enhance, broaden, and expand one's clinical work. "It encourages us to see our patients as more fully human, and to be more fully human ourselves" (p.26). Remaining mindful of the patient's psychological well-being in psychotherapy is essential, as is understanding and exploring the fullness of their images, cognitions, and feelings.

When psychotherapy is provided and the erotic countertransference is concretized through sexual involvement, the therapeutic container is irreparably shattered, the therapeutic trust betrayed, and the patient is victimized or revictimized through the current violation. The sexual enactment becomes extremely damaging for the patient and is also damaging for the therapist personally, professionally, legally, ethically, and economically. Holroyd and Brodsky (1977) found that therapists who had sexualized therapy with one patient often repeated this behavior with others. In fact the behavior recurred in 80 percent of the cases. In another study Pope, Keith-Speigel, and Tabachnik (1986) found 86 percent of therapists who became sexually intimate with their patients did so once or twice, but 10 percent did so between three and ten times.

This issue is raised in order to bring light to the devastating outcomes of this behavior and to encourage therapists to turn to colleagues, consultants, supervisors, or distressed therapist assistance programs such as the Colleague Assistance and Support

Program within the California Psychological Association, to address their fears or ethical breaches prior to acting on them. Likewise, professionals are encouraged to become concerned and directly address their colleagues' diminished capacities and symptoms of impairment such as alcohol or drug addiction, faulty clinical judgment, untreated and debilitating emotional distress or mental disorder, isolating behaviors, burnout, and attentional or memory disturbances in the aim of preventing any further tragedies. All of us within this profession have a duty to our colleagues and patients, regardless of any reluctance to breach these topics.

Wounded Healer Archetype

In classical mythology the centaur Chiron, half horse-half human, was endowed with the gift of healing and initiated Asklepios. An important characteristic of Chiron was his woundedness. Although Zeus endowed him with the gift of healing, he was fated to be mortally wounded. Thus, rather than die from this mortal wound he was restored to his full health, but the restoration was an ongoing process since the wounding continually resumed its destructiveness.

This image of the wounded healer provides us with a template to understand the inevitability of our own wounding. It signals the importance of accepting and living with our own wounds and the need to focus on their healing. Another way to understand this myth is to see our wounds as providing us with an entrance into a deep understanding of the suffering and pain that is part of our human nature, allowing us to empathize with others more easily, and possibly giving us a window into healing. The wound serves as a great teacher. To elaborate further, the myth speaks to the divine interventions that are needed for our healing to occur. Perhaps through mindful focusing, becoming aware of the meaning of the wound, experiencing the suffering emanating from the pain, and learning how to bear it, we create an opening for connecting to a divine healing potential, a source greater than our self. Sardello

(1988) recounted an experience he had while tending an illness "I believe there was importance in servicing the disease as my teacher. Medical diagnosis has the effect of isolation, of restricting one's illness in such a fashion that it is quite impossible to fully experience an illness as soul-making" (p. 15).

Last, Chiron's wound continued to wound him. The wounder and healer were one. This piece of the myth speaks to two issues: the inevitable wounding that we all participate in as humans, whether it is intentional, conscious, or unconscious and the internalized wounding that we may live with based on prior experiences of being harmed by others. The former aspect sheds light on accepting the imperfection that exists in human nature, and the need to take responsibility for our actions when we injure others. The latter speaks to the need for our own self awareness, growth, and continued individuation process. We need to work with our internal wounds, not only for our optimal health, but to impede the process of inadvertently hurting others from an unexamined place or crossing the well respected boundaries of the patient–therapist relationship. This has also been conceptualized as the management of risk factors within psychotherapy. I believe the consistent work with our own wounds respects our humanity as well as the importance of the work we engage in. The next chapter addresses the care of the therapeutic self in depth.

SIX

earth

Care of the Self

E lemental Earth lends the focus for this chapter. Earth represents the vital nurturance that accompanies our travels within psychological work and suggests the continued balance and replenishment we must attend to. Maintaining balance is a process that requires looking within, assessing the soil, taking time to regenerate for growth and fertility. This element is not seasonal but a consistent aspect of ensuring an ethical practice. It allows for a solid footing on the ground. Earth is represented by the closed circle that contains the balanced yin and yang symbols.

Self in Community

This chapter is devoted to the responsibilities centered on the therapeutic self, self in the context of Martin-Baro's (1994) expansive conceptualization of the communitarian self. He spoke of the receptive and egalitarian aspect of the self as an opening "toward the other, a readiness to let oneself be questioned by the other, as a separate being, to listen to his or her words, in dialogue; to confront reality in relationship to and with (but not over) him or her, to unite in solidarity in a struggle in which both will be transformed" (p.183).

Viewing self-care in this context is a way to integrate back into the community, to underscore the fluid connections to others, and to see the self as truly situated within community. The notion of self-care becomes a commitment and responsibility toward maintaining community. This is consistent with the Taoist that self is other.

Erosions of Empathy

We are trained to be empathically available to patients and may even suffer with patients "the sympathia" (von Franz, 1980, p.68). The capacity for empathy is integral to this profession, as the capacity for self-care is essential to a therapist's emotional competence (Koocher & Keith-Spiegel, 1998). Emotional competence is required in order to successfully contain and tolerate difficult clinical material, to assess bias, and to become aware of those anxiety-provoking experiences that signal one's subtle transgressions. Empathic or compassionate engagement may slowly shift or erode due to the context of the work. Witnessing compound losses and immense suffering through our work with children, adults, couples, and families who have experienced trauma can prove to be very challenging.

Once aware of these erosions or unsettling changes, we can employ heuristic methods (Moustakas, 1990) to investigate and discover the particularities. This involves self-search, self-dialogue, and self-discovery. Many theoretical formulations have been proposed to describe the constellation of responses professionals experience. The concepts of burnout, secondary traumatization, compassion fatigue, and vicarious traumatization attempt to capture the phenomenological experiences of professionals who work in this field.

"Burnout"

Burnout (Freudenberger, 1974) describes the physical, emotional, and mental exhaustion that impacts professionals in the negative manner in which they perceive self and other including colleagues and patients (Maslach, 1982). Burnout may develop insidiously and be unconscious. It is associated with a progressive deterioration in energy level resulting in extreme fatigue and a diminishment of one's prior idealism. It often occurs over a length of time where one is chronically exposed to stressors, but it can also develop from intensive concentrated activity. Emotional exhaustion is prominent, depersonalization in the treatment of patients, and the lack of a sense of personal competence in the face of stress are the factors frequently associated with burnout.

Compassion Fatigue

The concept of compassion fatigue has been addressed in the traumatic stress literature by Figley (1995). Compassion fatigue is an acute reaction manifesting in physical or mental exhaustion. This exhaustion impacts one's ability to express empathy or compassion and has been categorized as a form of burnout developing into secondary traumatic stress (Stebnicki, 2000). Unlike burnout, compassion fatigue does not deter most therapists from working, rather, the work is continued while the empathic capacities further erode. From the perspective of eros, one experiences *erosion*, a loss of connectedness and passion.

Vicarious Traumatization

Pearlman and Saakvitne (1995) developed the term vicarious traumatization to refer to therapists' responses and reactions to their work across time and across patients. Their focus was originally on the therapist treating patients working through issues of incest. "We do not believe anyone, however psychologically healthy, can do this work and remain unchanged" (p.295). Over the days, weeks, months, and years of doing this work, listening deeply, empathically engaging, confronting, containing uncomfortable material, and assisting with problem solving, the therapist is affected, over time, across patients. This impact on values, beliefs, and worldview can occur for therapists treating other populations as well. For some therapists, this may result in a slow, debilitating disempowerment, for others a hubris, no longer seeking consultation from others, believing they have all the knowledge and insight needed to do the work successfully. Both of these extremes result in profound changes that lead to unfavorable consequences, personally and professionally.

Restoration

Becoming involved in activities of the professional community provides opportunities for collaboration, participant sharing, and leads to the formation of an extended network of colleagues. Addressing and preventing burnout, compassion fatigue, and vicarious traumatization may involve joining a professional association (see Resources), becoming familiar with the monthly literature, reading journals, attending conferences or workshops, and seeking consultation or engaging in personal psychotherapy when faced with the inevitable discomfort that may accompany some of the therapeutic work. Participating in peer groups such as supportive weekly consultations, vicarious traumatization groups (Pearlman & Saakvitne, 1995), lunchtime support gatherings, and clinical supervision have also been recommended.

The institutionalization of mentoring programs for newer members of the profession is a unique way to support therapists in their professional development over time, effectively modeling a range of beneficial coping mechanisms. From a self-psychological perspective (Kohut, 1984) modeling can lead to the process known as transmuting internalization, or simply stated, integrating one's therapist or supervisor as a self-object. Holding an internal therapist or internal supervisor (Casement, 1991) can provide an extremely helpful referent in some circumstances. An active and effective internal supervisor is vital to our work, continually enhanced or modified based on successive experiences.

The erosion of connectedness, passion, and loving energy must be addressed. Referring to the process of restoration Leonard (1989) reminds us "accept the descent into the dark abyss, acknowledge the fall to the bottom . . . surrender to the greater powers that be" (p.243). The process of surrender may be extremely painful and difficult to experience, but may also initiate our own healing. I conclude with words from Rainer Maria Rilke's (1984) counsel to a young poet: "for these are the moments when something new has entered us, something unknown, and the new which no one knows, stands in the midst of it, and is silent" (p.74).

Care of The Self

Appreciating the mysteries in life, thriving in relationships, participating in vital activity within our communities are all life sustaining involvements. Cultivating a sacredness toward these daily activities is care of the soul (Moore, 1992). Therapist self-care is another facet of tending soul. It is curiously viewed as an innovative topic in clinical practice yet is necessary to ethical practice. The standard of self-care evolved from the theory that lack of self-care leads to ethical and legal transgressions, including boundary violations such as dual relationships (Lerman & Rigby, 1990). Recognizing and acknowledging personal limitations and seeking assistance is generally seen as a sign of strength, contributing to a therapist's growth and professionalism. In this context, self-care serves three primary functions: protects the patient by reducing risk factors, models growth and well-being, and protects the therapist against miscalculations and burnout (Porter, 1995).

As mentioned earlier, Pope and Brown (1996) conceptualized two types of therapeutic competence: intellectual and emotional competence. Intellectual competence is the knowledge and experiential base, including the assessment, treatment, and intervention skills possessed by the therapist. This area is traditionally encompassed by one's scope of education, training, and experience. Emotional competence refers to the ability to contain and tolerate the range of clinical material that emerges in treatment (Koocher & Keith-Spiegel, 1998), the ability to assess one's bias, and the capacity to engage in self-care.

Situating the capacity for self-care alongside the central and necessary capacity for empathy within the psychological profession solidifies the importance of therapist self-care, diminishes the risk management emphasis, and highlights the duty we have to emotional competence as a prevention effort. Self-care can be further broadened beyond emotional competence, incorporating a striving for emotional, psychological, physical, and spiritual well-being. In light of the potential development of burnout (Freudenberger, 1974), the progression of compassion fatigue (Figley, 1995), or the inevitable changes from vicarious traumatization (Pearlman & Saakvitne, 1995), a focus on self-care is indispensable.

Criteria for psychological health have been proposed in the clinical literature (Kinnier, 1997). This includes self-acceptance, self-knowledge, confidence, self-control, a clear perception of reality, courage and resilience, balance and moderation, love of others, love of life, and purpose in life. Adapting to challenges, integrating balance into life, and rediscovering or finding meaning and satisfaction are essential ingredients to psychological health.

Active Engagement In Self-Care

Active engagement in self-care can provide balance in one's life, improvement in personal relationships, and a renewed commitment to one's vocation, chosen career, or community. A definitive focus on self-care integrates both external and internal realities, involving relationships and activities with friends, family, and colleagues, in addition to spiritually, physically, and psychologically enriching endeavors, such as creative and artistic activities or appreciations, i.e., drawing, painting, writing, sculpting, dance, movement, drama, music, connecting with nature, contemplation, and meditation. Taking breaks from the intensity of the work, refocusing one's vision and commitment, and actively engaging in stress management speak to this explicit focus.

Regaining One's Vision

A focus on self-care becomes paramount during times of inordinate stress. At times it may seem as though the work is too challenging, testing commitment, or confusing one's direction. One may experience life inside the darkness of the labyrinth, not knowing if one is traveling forward or backward, east or west. Seeking consultation, taking time away from the work, renewing one's spirit may all contribute to the restoration of one's initial vision. Shifting one's perspective of work as contemplative practice, where one provides service without a sacrifice of self may prove rejuvenating. Remaining open to the potential and excitement of learning from all experiences without judging them as difficulties, hardships, or impossible hurdles reframes the challenge. Shifting our imagination from fear toward a "perception of more beauty" (Sardello, 1999, p.209) may be one way to address this process.

It may be helpful to identify a vision of one's optimal professional life or flow (Csikszentmihaly, 1990) through visualization or guided imagery. If you like, take a few moments at this time to reflect on your original passion and excitement about the field of psychology. Think back to a time when you initially identified psychology as your profession, or when others in your life encouraged you to follow this path given your natural talent, compassion, or interest in people. Perhaps you recall the sense of vocation, a calling to do this work, and are able to identify a moment in time where this became very clear to you. Get back in touch with your early feelings, images, and thoughts about how you expected to apply your training and skills. During graduate school, as you learned about psychology, research, and psychotherapy in depth, you refined these aspirations and expectations. How does your current practice integrate your hopes, desires, and vision? What developments do you imagine will be ahead in your future? What steps will you take to implement your vision today?

Just as a labyrinth will eventually lead to light, this type of contemplation can provide insight and renewal. Attending to one's personal needs, exercise, scheduling time for enjoyable activities, spending quality moments with friends and family, engaging in humor, and restoring one's vision will all contribute to a greater sense of well-being.

Research and anecdotal reports indicate suggest animals can promote humor, laughter, and play in people (Cusack, 1988). Matthew Fox (1990) proposed a number of spiritual lessons we can learn from animals in his book *A Spirituality Named Compassion*. The lessons include:

The joy of being an animal;
Experiencing ecstasy without guilt;
Playing with no justification for the behavior;
Remaining open;
Exhibiting broadened sensitivity;

Humor, considered a:

"radical celebrative awareness of dialectic and paradox" (Fox, 1990, p.167);

The power of non-verbal communication;

The grace of beauty, sensuousness, and silent dignity in acknowledgment of one's self worth and pride. These are all valuable lessons to incorporate into our lives.

Self-Care and Coping with Stress

For the most part, stress is a companion to be embraced not defended against, for it is a natural response to threatening, difficult, or challenging events or circumstances. A survival mechanism that alerts us to danger and activates protective functions. Modern day stress also motivates, inspires, invigorates, and encourages us to develop our capacities. It may push us toward accomplishment in endeavors we might otherwise never attempt. Stress also maintains our awareness, contributes to alertness, and generally keeps us alive.

However, when stress becomes unrelenting, extreme, or chronic, its benefits recede being replaced by obstacles or impairments. Many of us are all too familiar with the physical and emotional toll chronic or excessive stress can take including the contributions to cardiovascular disease, interference with thought processes, cessation of creativity, disruption of relationships, prevention of sleep, and the development of addictive behavior. Conversely the absence of stress can be symptomatic as well, resulting in feelings of boredom, fatigue, apathy, loss of purpose or mission, and lack of challenge, and loss of flow.

The art of stress management is seeking a balance between the poles of stimulation and relaxation and taking responsibility for making beneficial changes and implementing stress reduction techniques. This becomes a unique process of discovery, focusing on what, when, how much, and how. Noticing what creates the stress and what the stressors are the initial steps in this process. Assessing the conditions, times of day, month, or season that contribute to the stress is the second step. Becoming aware of understimulation as well as the amount of stress that is optimal for one's functioning will reveals one's stress parameters. And last, exploring, investigating, and experimenting with effective stress reduction methods can present novel and relaxing experiences. These explorations can be quite enjoyable in and of themselves.

Recognizing that a stress reaction is one's personal response to a stressor or accumulation of stressors is essential, since stress is not the actual situation, such as a particular job, issue, role, supervisor, or patient. This recognition is supported by Frankl's (1994) severe experiences in concentration camps and his comment that one's attitude toward the incident or trauma is the factor that impacts one's ability to cope. This distinction speaks to the variability of human experience in that each one of us responds to stressors differently. Our personality characteristics, way of being, and access to support systems, and willingness to reach out for assistance all affect the way we respond to events.

Simple remedies exist for addressing stress on a daily basis. Taking a walk away from the chaos in one's office or job can provide moments of awe strolling through a garden, a park, or down a path. Stopping to watch birds, experiencing the scent of a flower, gazing up into the sky, or noticing the breeze on one's neck are all ways to open up the senses differently. Deep breathing techniques serve calming functions and may be integrated into brief interludes during one's day. Laughter or laughing robustly energizes and may release boredom or apathy, shifting the previous physiological sensations. Taking a few minutes to meditate or focus oneself on a task while letting go of all other concerns can lead to clarity when stepping back to the previous work. Marge Piercy's (2000) poem *On Six Underrated Pleasures* listed a number of activities that could relieve stress: folding sheets, picking pole beans, taking a hot bath, sleeping with cats, planting bulbs, and canning!

Reaching out to friends and colleagues for support in the form of a phone call, tea break, or sharing a meal rather than consistently isolating oneself, can be very comforting in times of stress, moments of judgment, confusion, or fear. Taking time to deeply listen to another person in a conversation can also decrease frustrations or stresses. Similarly, attending to the needs of something or someone else or working in a garden allows for moments of other-directed care that replenish and revitalize.

Participating in a class that ordinarily is considered trivial could expand one's repertoire of self-care. Scheduling body work, massage, or other forms of physical touch can soothe tight muscles and provide physical relaxation. Choosing foods that support your well being, exercising, and participating in group activities with friends all increase the likelihood of health. And of course limiting work activities, prioritizing time, not overscheduling one's life, and holding commitments to a minimum during stressful times shows kindness and acknowledgment of one's humanness.

Engaging in creativity can be a delightful stress release. In her Jungian story telling series, Estes (1991) likened creativity to the physiological processes associated with nourishment, elimination, and the production of excrement. She alluded to the life sustaining nutrients the body requires and the daily toxicity that builds up if not released. Similarly, creativity moves through, provides nourishment, energy, life-giving properties, and moves onward to liberation or expression. If the eliminatory processes are restricted, the toxicity begins to build up within the body. Once liberated the resulting material may serve as a kind of regenerating fertilizer. Imagine conceptualizing acts of creativity as daily and necessary activities for health, both mental and physical.

Affirmations of creativity can be experienced in peaceful and inspiring moments of artistic self-expression in the form of journal writing, sculpting, drawing, movement, preparing a meal, or sitting down in silence to write a letter. Crafting a novel, short story, or a song for the enjoyment of expression can be exhilarating.

Creating Space and Reframing

Creating a special place within your imagination, home, office, or outdoors in a park, on a special bench, under a masterful tree, associates one's contemplative time with this special or sacred place. Reframing the way one thinks about certain stressors may also successfully eliminate the perceived burden. Scaling down the importance or severity of some incidents may be more manageable.

Managing Stress–The Meridian Assessment Paradigm

Enlisting the Meridian Assessment Paradigm (Lipinski, 2001b) as a self-assessment "M.A.P." of stress management is a systematic way to promote well being, shift one's usual cadence, and attenuate potentially debilitating stress. The following model synthesizes awareness, evaluation, and implementation.

Matter

Begin with an assessment of the body or matter (*L.* mater). Notice what parts of the body are most in need of attention. The presence of health, illness, and specific symptoms causing distress or pain are worth noting and addressing through medical attention, holistic intervention, and prevention. Focus on nurturing one's body and opening up the senses through massage, aromatherapy, use essential oils, engage in bodywork, listen to enjoyable sounds and music, obtain relaxing recordings, alter the diet, and follow-through on physical examinations. Become aware of your sleeping patterns and sleep hygiene, noticing the quality of sleep obtained and whether you are refreshed each morning. Consult with a specialist on sleep disorders if you suspect a problem. Cook a new recipe, exercise in a different style, engage in a sport, or begin a new well-being program incorporating a physical health perspective.

Ecological

Span your landscape, the territory you dwell in, and assess the elements that contribute or detract from your psychological health and well-being. Evaluate aspects you have control over and prioritize changing these: perhaps an eventual move to another environment, a job enhancement, an economic investment, consultation with a financial advisor, or packing some possessions for contribution to a charitable organization. Participate in the community in a different way becoming involved in community organization, recycling, or grass roots political efforts. Getting back in touch with nature by spending time strolling, hiking, camping, or allowing quality time with wild animals or companions all address this ecological dimension. Touch back with your childlike self to remember wonder and curiosity. At times simply watching fish swim, listening to songbirds, or sitting among flowers endows well-being. Energizing one's space through redecoration, furniture rearrangement, or consultation with a feng shui practitioner may create delightful shifts.

Relational

Notice the interpersonal relationships within your life, the level of satisfaction, the amount of extroversion, and quality of nurturance you experience and provide. Assess the ways you can improve and deepen these valuable connections. Examine the relationships with co-workers, family, friends, and acquaintances. Notice the relationships with ancestors or the recently deceased. Discuss ways of enhancing your intimate relationships, improving sexual expression, and quality of companionship. Perhaps engaging in new adventures, family therapy, or a self-help group would contribute to enhancement. Renew old friendships, nurture new acquaintances, and acknowledge strangers differently within your life. Focus on enhancing and improving the "in between."

Interiority

Assess the intrapersonal dimension of life. Become aware of the time you allow for introversion and focus on your interior life. Notice the quality of your intrapersonal relationship and whether you permit sufficient time for a rich interior life. Appraise the predominant mood, feelings, and rhythm you regularly experience. Create moments within your schedule for solitude, contemplation, meditation, and journaling. Engage in psychotherapy, experiment with silence, yoga, or become involved in a personal growth class. Read a memoir, science fiction, romance, or a thrilling novel. Devote time to a life inventory assessing the aspects of life you are pleased with, noting the developmental phase you are in, thinking through your life mission, and creating future goals, objectives, or direction. Listen to your intuition about these precious aspects of your life.

Deportment

Although an old term, *deportment* speaks clearly to this highly visible yet often neglected dimension. Take stock in your overall demeanor, personal, and professional behavior. Imagine what friends and acquaintances see through your behavior and carriage of your unique body. Elicit feedback from others on this point. Note the way you carry your body, grimace or smile, and fully experience this aspect of yourself from head to toe. Imagine ways to change or improve the way you hold yourself or let yourself go via musculature or tension. Become aware of your gestures, movements, tone and pitch of voice, and fluidity of walking. Attend to any repetitive or compulsive behaviors.

Begin to bring the outward image you project in line with your interior sense of self. This may include an integration of new movements, participation in personal life coaching sessions, or acquiring a different wardrobe that is more personally and uniquely expressive. Involvement in postural improvements, integrating a yoga practice, learning the balanced meditative movements of Tai Chi, bodywork, synergy, or integrative body structuring may be rejuvenating.

Imaginal

Begin to notice the quality of your imaginal life and how you attend to or neglect it. Begin to tend dreams, notice waking dreams, amplify spontaneous images, review thoughts, and augment your artistic expression. Create time to consciously and intentionally engage the figures and characters of your imagination. Energizing this aspect of existence encompasses interior, relational, and behavioral methods. Partaking of community festivals, art shows, dramatic performances, concerts, and art museum exhibitions magnify imaginal life. Employ active imagination to engage dream figures or images. Create a sand painting or mandala, a figure from clay, a mask, drawing, poem, or simply play to enliven your imaginal life. Enlarge the experience by entertaining or involving colleagues and friends.

Archetypal

Begin to look at your life as personal mythology. Notice the universal patterns, the recurring symbols, the invisible, the muted, the subtle, and any predominant themes. Who visits in this drama? Notice the other characters within your drama, epic, comedy, tragedy, or lyric. Discover what has been neglected or unseen. Perhaps reading more mythology, attending a class, consulting with archetypal psychologists will reveal more.

Numinous

Become aware of the level of your spiritual or religious practice. Assess ways to strengthen this facet of your life, perhaps integrating religious observances, praying, reading more literature, or renewing attendance at church, synagogue, or temple. Recall any recent synchronicities or coincidental experiences. Remember the times you experienced epiphanies and what conditions were present in your life. Seek spiritual consultation, participate in oracular divination methods, or engage in an astrological reading. Make a commitment to a practice that is aligned with your beliefs, passions, and interests.

Concluding Comment on Self-care

When involved in a preparation process for an oral or written exam, a focus on self-care is necessary. Attending to one's personal needs, exercise, making time for enjoyable activities, spending quality moments with friends and family, will all contribute to your preparation. Maintaining a sense of humor can also be energizing. Adopting this integrative perspective will help manage your time. Reducing overall physical anxiety will decrease the additional physiological arousal that often accompanies test taking situations.

Procrastination is often a common defense against these fears and anxieties that emerge. In fact, I have known many therapists who had spotless vehicles, well planted gardens, and extremely clean homes during their studying process! If you find yourself engaging in these types of activities, acknowledge them as being within a normal range, allow yourself to engage in them, but perhaps on a Premack principle, where you promise yourself that activity after studying for a certain length of time. The paradoxical nature of this intervention might be one way to rediscover your motivation. Using other methods to directly limit, reduce, or minimize anxiety may be necessary, such as time limited studying, studying with a reliable partner, video or audiotaping yourself, relaxation training, guided imagery, behavioral rehearsal of the exam situation, biofeedback, and psychotherapy. And last, taking stock in all you already know will help you affirm your competence in this field. The task ahead is to enhance your skills to confidently articulate the depth of your knowledge to examiners, who are ultimately your peers.

PART III

courage

CENTERING THE DYNAMICS OF PRACTICE

SEVEN

harmony

Back to Beginnings

Part Three acknowledges the importance of centering these dynamics of clinical practice in the Tao of integrity. This chapter begins with the character for Harmony representing the professional spirit that underlies the initiation of a psychotherapeutic relationship. The arrangement of the various parts necessary for the whole, such as confidentiality, informed consent, and even the advertising process are important elements in an ethical practice. Equivalents of harmony stir up images of the balance or equilibrium between yin and yang, the active and receptive, the linear and spiral. An awareness of the required structure, the general standards, and an openness to considerations that are unique to a specific case or patient are considered in this realm. Courage is also called upon in the work within psychotherapy, noted within Part III.

The most prominent and highly referenced ethical and legal issues integral to beginning the psychotherapeutic process are presented: advertising, concurrent treatment, confidentiality, fees and insurance issues, informed consent, privileged communications, record keeping guidelines, and services to minors. Studying these will provide a basis for the ethical framework embodied within psychotherapeutic practice. Seasoned practitioners will find these issues merit revisiting and contribute to an ongoing integration process.

Ethical Standards

Ethical standards and aspirational goals are promulgated by professional associations such as the American Psychological Association, American Association for Marriage and Family Therapists, American Counseling Association, and California Association for Marriage and Family Therapists. The APA is currently revising the ethical standards that have been in place since 1992 in order to update the language and augment the principles and standards. The revised code (American Psychological Association, 2001) has five general aspirational principles: A) Beneficence and non-maleficence; B) Fidelity and social responsibility; C) Integrity; D) Justice; and E) Respect for people's rights ad dignity. The standards address eleven issues including the resolution of ethical issues, competence, human relations, privacy and confidentiality, advertising and other public representations, record keeping and fees, teaching and training supervision, research and publication, assessment, therapy, and forensic activities. The code does not apply to a psychologist's private conduct but applies to all professional activities. This is the scientific, educational, and professional activities psychologists engage in and includes multiple contexts such as services delivered by phone, electronically, and in face to face personal contacts.

Advertising

Psychotherapists may engage in informational activities to enable individuals to choose psychotherapeutic services. Professional organizations and state licensing laws usually set forth standards for proper advertising and promotional activities. Provisions and interpretations are summarized below.

Advertisements are to be accurate and truthful representation of relevant competence, education, training, and experience; only claiming a specialization if related training, education and supervised experience meet recognized professional standards; not misrepresenting qualifications of trainees, interns, or other associates. Psychotherapists are also responsible for information that appears within an advertisement and should take appropriate action to make clarifications or corrections when necessary.

Advertisements are crafted to furnish sufficient and clear information for the public to make an appropriate selection. This may include name, address, telephone number, fee structure, relevant degrees, state licenses, description of specialty or practice, and professional association membership. If you use the term psychotherapist to describe your practice, include either the full name of your licensure or license number (California Code of Regulations Title 16, § 1811), since the professions of marriage and family therapy, psychology, and social work may all practice psychotherapy. Omitting this information is considered misleading.

Advertising-Inappropriate Conduct

Inappropriate conduct includes using a false or misleading business name; making false public statements; making any claim or statement that is false, misleading, or deceptive, or encouraging or allowing patients to have false or exaggerated expectations regarding the services offered. If you are a therapist in training, your advertisements should indicate this along with your supervisor's name and license number.

Concurrent Treatment from Other Therapists

The intention is to act in accordance with the best interests of the patient. Depending on the circumstances, it may or may not be unethical to see a patient who is concurrently seeing one or more other therapists. A therapist should carefully consider the treatment issues and the potential patient's welfare. The therapist discusses these issues with the patient in order to minimize the risk of confusion and conflict, consults with the other therapists when appropriate. Many recommend proceeding with caution and sensitivity to the therapeutic issues.

If a patient is concurrently seeing one or more therapists, and it is determined that therapy with you is in the patient's best interests, you may proceed with the therapy. Some examples include: The patient is in individual therapy with you and in couple's therapy with another provider, or is receiving issue specific therapy (e.g. systematic desensitization for a phobia) elsewhere outside the scope of your training or experience.

If a patient is in therapy with another therapist and appears to be hiding this fact from his or her other therapist, it is unethical to continue seeing the patient if there was no apparent therapeutic benefit. In a complex situation like this, it is important to raise the issue, explain the ethics of the situation, seek to illuminate the patient's motives and intentions in working with another therapist, and encourage direct discussion with the original therapist, if at all possible.

Confidentiality

The ethical and legal responsibility to maintain the confidentiality of patient-psychotherapist communications, including the fact that a particular person is or is not a patient, is essential both to the effectiveness of therapy and the patient's safety and well-being. Confidentiality is considered a foundational and necessary element in psychotherapy, and builds on the right of privacy, going "beyond that afforded by the federal constitution" (Caudill & Pope, 1995, p. 166). Professional associations, licensing boards, and legal statutes all provide severe consequences for unauthorized disclosures, such as disciplinary action, expulsion from professional membership (Mills, 1984), censure, reprimand (Hall & Hare-Mustin, 1983), revocation of license to practice, and civil or criminal penalties. The ultimate consequence is the betrayal perpetrated by the therapist upon the patient.

Information disclosed by a patient to a psychotherapist, covered by the psychotherapist-patient privilege, is considered confidential. However, since privilege is established by statute and case law, some communications are not privileged. Refer to the information on Privilege within this text for further information on the limitations of the scope of privilege.

Confidential communication between patient and psychotherapist is defined in Evidence Code Section 1012. The following is an excerpt: "information obtained by an examination of the patient, transmitted between a patient and his psychotherapist in the course of that relationship and in confidence by a means which, so far as the patient is aware, discloses the information to no third persons other than those who are present to further the interest of the patient in the consultation, or those to whom disclosure is reasonably necessary for the transmission of the information or the accomplishment of the purpose for which the psychotherapist is consulted, and includes a diagnosis made and the advice given by the psychotherapist in the course of that relationship." Even with the legally permitted consultation noted in the last part of this definition, it is considered sensible ethical practice to obtain a written consent from the patient, delineating the specific information that will be shared or sought. "Obtaining written consent helps promote clarity of communication between therapist and client in situations when misunderstandings can be disastrous" (Pope & Vasquez, 1998, p. 226).

Despite the validity of confidentiality as both an ethical and legal mandate, it is disregarded intentionally and unintentionally far too often. Pope & Bajt (1988) reported confidentiality was the most frequent intentional ethical and legal violation by participants in their national study. Pope, Tabachnick, & Keith-Spiegel (1987) reported over half of the respondents in their study unintentionally violated patient confidentiality.

Under most circumstances confidential information should not be released without the explicit written consent of the patient. However, in certain circumstances, confidentiality must be or may be breached.

These circumstances are:

1) Those in which a therapist is legally mandated to breach confidentiality (must be breached), and

2) Those in which a therapist is legally permitted but not obligated to do so (may be breached).

In those cases where a mandate to disclose confidential information exists, an ethical and well educated psychotherapist remembers to disclose only to the extent required by law. This means providing the limited necessary information, but nothing more. For this reason, keeping abreast of the relevant statutes affecting the practice of psychotherapy is crucial. If you are in doubt about required or permissible breaches, seek consultation immediately, to protect both the patient and yourself. The intention is to minimize inadvertent and improper disclosure. "Willful, unauthorized communication of information received in professional confidence" (Business & Professions Code § 2960) is considered unprofessional conduct.

<u>Situations in which Confidentiality Must be Breached</u>

♦ Tarasoff–Duty to Warn–If in the course of therapy, a patient has communicated to the psychotherapist a serious threat of physical violence against a reasonably identifiable victim or victims, the therapist must make reasonable efforts to communicate the threat to the victim(s) and to a law enforcement agency (Tarasoff v Regents of the University of California, Civil Code 43.92).

♦ Child Abuse Reporting–When a therapist, in his or her professional capacity, knows or reasonably suspects that a child is being abused, he or she is legally obligated to make a report to a child protective agency (Penal Code § 11166).

♦ Dependent Adult and Elder Abuse–When a therapist, in his or her professional capacity, has observed an incident that reasonably appears to be physical abuse, has observed a physical injury which indicates that there has been abuse, is told by an elder or dependent adult that abuse has occurred, or reasonably suspects dependent adult or elder abuse, the therapist is required to report that abuse to an adult protective agency (Welfare and Institutions Code § 15630).

♦ Court Orders: When a court has recognized an exception to privilege and ordered the release of records or a therapist's testimony, the individual must release the records or appear for testimony.

♦ *Assault or abuse: There is no longer any law requiring psycho-therapists to breach confidentiality in cases of spousal assault or abuse. For a brief period of time, it had been required, then repealed. However, it was limited to those working in a clinic, health facility, or physician's office.*

Situations in Which Confidentiality May Be Breached
Breach is permissible

♦ Patient is a Danger to Self, Others, or Property (with no third-party identifiable victim involved). As per Evidence Code Section 1024, when the psychotherapist has reasonable cause to believe that a person is in such mental or emotional condition as to be dangerous to her or "himself or to the person or property of another <u>and</u> that disclosure of the communication is necessary to prevent the threatened danger" (emphasis added), a breach of confidentiality is permitted e.g., calling the police, a friend, the Psychiatric Assessment Team. This may include threats of suicide. Please see section on Suicidal Ideation in chapter eleven.

♦ Patient is Gravely Disabled due to a mental disorder. When a patient is not competent to take reasonably good care of herself or himself, (assessed in the areas of food, clothing, and shelter,) a therapist may ethically breach confidentiality if reasonably providing for the health and welfare of the patient (Welfare and Institutions Code 5150).

♦ Non-Mandated Elder or Dependent Adult Abuse Reporting. When the criteria for a mandated report are not met, a report is optional. The law does not currently specify what these categories of abuse may be, however, an important element is the elder or dependent adult's emotional well-being is endangered. Clearly this requires an evaluation of the situation based on one's professional judgment.

Office Policies Form and Confidentiality

Before psychotherapy begins, it is wise to provide an office policies form or therapeutic contract as part of gaining informed consent, including a brief outline of situations in which confidentiality must and may be breached. Such a form can help to reduce the problems associated with mandated or optional breaches of confidentiality. Having a document such as this can prove invaluable if and when situations arise where confidentiality may or must be breached. The document may be reviewed during psychotherapy as well. This would also help you meet the ethical obligation of informing patients of the legal limits of confidentiality.

Fees, Fee Setting, and Insurance Reimbursement

Several issues are involved with the concept of fees, including setting a fee, when to discuss the fee, insurance issues, and bill collecting. "When finances are brought up in the course of a psychologist's formal training, specific discussion of actual practices involving billing, collection, and third-party reimbursement are rarely mentioned" (Koocher & Keith-Spiegel, 1998, p.234). The successful independent practice of psychotherapy requires the appropriate management of these issues. Insurance issues are addressed in the following section.

Fee Setting

As early as is possible, the therapist and patient should reach an agreement specifying the compensation including the billing arrangement–preferably during first contact, e.g., telephone call or intake session–so patient may decide to proceed based on informed consent. If limitations to services can be anticipated because of limitations in financing, this is discussed with the patient as early as possible. One approach is to charge the prevailing rate in the community, and maintain some low cost hours for a few patients who either can't afford full fee, or who suffer financial difficulties during on-going therapy. In order to learn about the prevailing rate, consult with colleagues and your professional association regarding recent surveys on independent practice. For example, *The California Association for Marriage and Family Therapists* makes available periodic survey information indicating the geographic regional differences in fees, including the customary and prevailing rates.

When Fee Is Not Affordable

You are not legally or ethically compelled to see patients for free unless there are special circumstances such as a crisis situation which you see the patient through. Financial issues should not take precedence over a patient's welfare. It is improper to simply abandon an existing patient because she/he cannot pay your fee. If the patient is in crisis, it may be important to see the patient through the crisis before terminating. You may work out a mutually agreeable arrangement with the patient, such as meeting less frequently or for a lower fee. Provide potential or actual patient with low or no cost referrals if it is not feasible for you to be the therapist.

Non-Payment of Fees

You may not withhold records that are later requested solely because payment has not been received. The patient's welfare takes precedence over financial issues. In circumstances where the patient has not paid the agreed upon fee, a collection agency may be utilized after you have exhausted all other means of collection and the patient has been informed the account will be turned over to a collection agency. Only information relevant to collecting payment may be released in these instances.

Insurance Issues

In instances when patients have insurance coverage for psychotherapy, the fee is agreed to in advance (as with other patients) and charges must be billed appropriately and ethically. An important ethical principle here involves non-exploitation and integrity. The decision as to who receives the billing is made by the therapist and patient (unless a managed care company is involved and has specific requirements): it is acceptable to bill either the patient or insurance company directly.

Billing should clearly reflect the specific services provided, the disorders being treated, as well as the co-payment received. For example, telephone sessions need to be indicated as such, not listed as an individual psychotherapy session within the office.

Insurance bills should indicate customary fees. An unethical practice is to create a bill reflecting a higher fee than regularly charged for that specific service. Whenever fees are adjusted, the bill reflects this activity, even when the result is a lower payment from the insurance provider.

Insurance Co-Payment

Good-faith attempts to collect the patient's co-payment portion of fees are required. When acting in good faith, in some instances, the psychotherapist may eventually be faced with writing off the patient's unpaid portion of fees at the conclusion of therapy.

With a cancellation or unexpected missed appointment, the insurance company may not be billed, since services were not delivered. This issue is preferably addressed with the patient during the initial stage of psychotherapy as part of gaining informed consent. Often the therapist informs the patient of the expectations and responsibilities regarding cancellations.

It is considered ethically responsive to reduce the total fees when a patient experiences a financial crisis. A mutually agreed upon fee affordable for the patient is in the best interest of the patient.

Informed Consent and Assent

Many years ago, in the times of Hippocrates, health practitioners were advised to conceal procedures from the patient. "Perform all this calmly and adroitly, concealing most things from the patient while you are attending to him" (as cited in O'Neill, 1998, p.10). Fortunately, the times have changed in favor of patients' rights. Thus the current standard emphasizes the affirmative duty of the psychotherapist to inform the patient about the treatment process including the possible shortcomings and risks.

Informed consent took seed in the Salgo v. Stanford University (1957) case in which the phrase was coined. Since that time many cases have brought further clarity to this concept. Currently, the widely accepted procedure is threefold:

1) provide the patient with significant information concerning psychotherapy, provided the patient has the capacity to consent,

2) obtain the patient's freely expressed consent, and

3) document the consent in the patient record.

INFORMED CONSENT PROCESS

PROVIDE INFORMATION
OBTAIN CONSENT
DOCUMENT

If the patient is not legally capable of giving informed consent, the practitioner should provide information about the "proposed interventions in a manner commensurate with the persons' psychological capacities" (APA, 1992, standard 4.02c) and seek assent to the interventions. Consent should be obtained from a legally authorized person, as permitted by law.

In many professional association's codes, such as the American Counseling Association's Code of Ethics and Standards of Practice, practitioners are encouraged to make full disclosures to patients, both at the initiation of the work and during the work. This is a very realistic standard for the psychotherapy process since the issues of time and duration play a significant role. Pope and Vasquez (1991) state "As the treatment plan undergoes significant evolution, the patient must adequately understand these changes and voluntarily agree to them" (p.75).

What type of therapeutic information is disclosed with the intent of informed consent? "Counselors inform clients of the purposes, goals, techniques, procedures, limitations, potential risks, and benefits of services to be performed, and other pertinent information. Counselors take steps to ensure that clients understand the implications of diagnosis, the intended use of tests and reports, fees, and billing arrangements" (National Board of Certified Counselors, 1997, Section B8). Additionally, O'Neill (1998) believes that specific information about alternative treatments should be included even if they are out of the therapist's scope of training and experience, thus necessitating a referral.

Privileged Communications

Psychotherapist-patient communications are considered privileged communications. Patients can freely express themselves, describing the problems and issues they are facing in an honest and open manner. The privilege can benefit and protect the patient, however it does not offer protection in all instances. Limitations on the scope of the privilege are covered later in this section. A communication considered privileged is a "communication that the holder of the privilege must authorize disclosure of and testimony about" (Caudill & Pope, 1995, p. 171). The psychotherapist-patient privilege is codified by statute, which means it is defined by law.

Privilege of Confidentiality Rule

The focus here is within the context of legal proceedings where attempts are made to have the content of confidential patient therapist communications revealed. No disclosure can properly be made by the therapist to anyone else unless there is an appropriate waiver of the privilege or the privilege is limited by an exception.

Who May Assert to Waive the Privilege

Privilege may only be asserted or waived by the holder of the privilege. This is usually the patient, but under Evidence Code 1015 the psychotherapist is required to assert the privilege, to "claim" the privilege on the patient's behalf, when a party attempts to have a psychotherapist reveal the content of a patient's communication in a legal proceeding. Without an appropriate waiver, the sought after information remains confidential, and is not subject to disclosure.

Waiver of Privilege

Patient may waive the privilege. There is no privilege if it has been waived by the patient (the holder of the privilege). If a patient wishes to have the patient-therapist communications disclosed in a legal proceeding, the therapist cannot prevent him or her from doing so.

Please remember that the patient, *even if a minor*, is generally the holder of the privilege. The Evidence Code names only three holders of the privilege, one of which is a *legal guardian*. It is important to note that a parent may or may not be a legal guardian, but would need to be designated so in order to hold the privilege for a minor.

THREE HOLDERS OF THE PRIVILEGE

1. The patient;
2. Legal guardian or conservator of the patient;
3. Personal representative of the patient if the patient is deceased.

Limitations to Privilege

The following limitations to privilege illustrate the range of situations that require or permit the disclosure of confidential communications. These are most common to the psychotherapist-patient relationship. All are set forth in the California Evidence Code. Readers interested in other exceptions are referred to Evidence Code Section 1017, court appointed evaluator; Section 1019, parties claiming through deceased patient; Section 1021, intention of deceased patient concerning writing affecting property interest; Section 1022, validity of writing affecting property interest; Section 1026, required report to public employee.

1. Patient under 16, victim of crime.

There is no privilege if the patient is a child under 16, and the psychotherapist has reasonable cause to believe that the patient has been the victim of a crime and that disclosure of the communication is in the best interest of the child (Evidence Code § 1027).

2. Dangerous patient exception.

There is no privilege under Evidence Code Section 1024. Patient is dangerous to himself or others or property of others and therapist has reasonable cause to believe this is the case, and the disclosure is necessary to prevent the threatened danger. This law is broader than the other exceptions to privilege, in that, besides applying to legal proceedings, it also applies to the clinical setting.

3. Crime or tort.

There is no privilege if the patient sought therapy to aid in planning, committing, escaping punishment, detection, or apprehension regarding a crime or tort (Evidence Code § 1018).

4. Patient-Litigant exception.

There is no privilege when the patient's emotional condition is raised as an issue by patient or his/her representative, examples include a worker's compensation suit regarding stress, a proceeding to determine sanity in a criminal action suit, or proceedings to establish competence (Evidence Code § 1016).

5. Breach of Duty.
(Arising Out of Psychotherapist-Patient Relationship).

There is no privilege when either a psychotherapist or patient alleges a breach of duty arising out of the psychotherapist-patient relationship (e.g., within a malpractice lawsuit). This law has limited applicability outside the context of legal proceedings, e.g., if a patient refuses to pay his or her bill for therapy, the therapist may reveal information relevant to collecting payment (i.e., the patient's name and address and the amount owed), but no other information, to a collection agencies should notify patients of this practice at the outset of therapy (Evidence Code § 1020).

6. Proceeding to Establish Competence.

There is no privilege in a proceeding brought by or on behalf of the patient to establish his competence (Evidence Code § 1025). Competence hearings focus on capacities to understand, to act reasonably, to carry out duties.

7.   Proceeding to Determine Sanity.

There is no privilege in a proceeding to determine a patient's sanity (Evidence Code § 1023). Insanity is a complex legal term signifying lack of criminal responsibility to some degree.

8.   Court or Legally Mandated Disclosure.

Examples include: Reporting child, dependent adult, or elder abuse (see Welfare and Institutions Code § 15632a); These are restricted disclosures. Fortunately, child abuse, dependent adult abuse, and elder abuse reports are themselves confidential (Penal Code § 11166; Welfare and Institutions Code § 15630-15631).

Record Keeping Guidelines

Acting in a professional manner requires keeping some basic patient records and notes concerning patients' biographical, residential, employment, and related basic information; as well as legally required entries such as indicating the reason a minor was treated without parental consent and the efforts made to contact the parents if appropriate. Knowing the documentation requirements of the institution in which one works is also essential. Additional reasons for records and notes include:

a)   Treatment continuity provided by the therapist;
b)   Helping transition to other therapists, or when
      patient returns to therapy after a substantial time gap;
c)   Verification of mental status for disability, insurance
      company requirements, and workers' compensation
      claims;
d)   A resource for future research, writing, or teaching;
e)   Liability protection if therapist is called upon to
      justify treatment (whether in a court case, lawsuit,
      or ethics committee investigation).

In fact when a psychologist knows the records will be subject to legal scrutiny, he or she is ethically bound to create records in the quality and detail that would be useful in the proceedings (APA, 1992, standard 1.23b). However, under some circumstances it may be in the best interests of the patient to limit the content of the notes and records. Keep in mind that whatever data or information is placed in patient notes and records is subject to potential full disclosure in some form of legal proceeding.

Content and Length of Records and Notes

No clear legal or ethical standards of practice speak to the overall content and length of patient records and notes. For the most part, these are discretionary decisions for the psychotherapist. Some practitioners favor lengthy and detailed notes; while others prefer brief and sketchy ones. The basic rule is *acting in the best interest of the patient*, and clearly reasonable minds may differ on what this requires.

Content of Records Minimally Include

Identifying data, dates of services, types of services, fees, any assessment, plan for intervention, consultation, summary reports, release of information documents, and testing reports (APA, 1993, 1B)

Access to Records and Notes

These confidential documents belong to the therapist, and should be kept in a locked, safe, and secure place. The therapist is responsible for the safety and confidentiality of the record. The patient has the right to request copies, and the therapist, for good reason can provide only a summary. If a patient insists on full access, and the therapist objects, mediation is the next level of response. Ultimately, if records and notes are subpoenaed, it is prudent to refuse access until ordered by a court to comply.

Providing Services to Minors

The following section presents ethical and legal aspects involved in the treatment of minors. Two important legal aspects are listed below:

♦ No minor under 12 can receive outpatient mental health counseling without parental consent.

♦ All minors who are emancipated can receive outpatient counseling without parental consent.

Minors–Confidentiality

Generally, minors (persons under age 18) are entitled to the protection of confidentiality unless there is an applicable legal or ethical exception. Exceptions are the same as with adult patients (e.g. threats of violence to another, or suicide; reporting abuse; patient gravely disabled; etc.). An additional exception is the right of parents to inspect the therapist's records concerning their child when the treatment is with parental consent. If full disclosure is not in the best interests of the minor patient, a therapist can provide a summary and use arbitration if necessary to determine minimum disclosure. If this proves unsatisfactory wait for court order to disclose more.

Privilege of Confidentiality

With respect to a situation in which a minor has requested and been given mental health treatment pursuant to an exception, the minor holds the privilege. This also applies if she or he is treated as an adult due to emancipation. *Evidence Code § 1014.5 was eliminated and is no longer specified in law–this referred to the psychotherapist holding the privilege. The patient has the right to assert Privilege as a means of blocking disclosure of confidential information during a court or other legal proceeding. The holder of the privilege has this right. If the minor has a court appointed legal guardian or conservator that individual becomes the holder of the privilege.

When Parental Consent is Required for Treatment

Consent must always be secured for treatment of individuals under 12 years of age.

Treatment of Minors Without Parental Consent

Treatment of minors without parental consent is legally permissible when the minor consents and is either legally emancipated or meets the criteria on an exception within specific preconditions and treatable clinical issues. However, when treating under an exception, parental consent must be obtained at any later time that is deemed appropriate.

Specific Preconditions & Treatable Clinical Issue(s) Exception

1. Preconditions Required:
    a) 12 or older;
    b) Sufficiently mature to participate intelligently;
    c) Therapy is on an outpatient basis; and
    d) Good reason for treating without parental consent.

2. Treatable Clinical Issue(s):
    a) Minor would present a danger of serious physical or mental harm to him/herself or to others without treatment. Family Code § 6924;
    b) Minor has been the alleged victim of incest or child abuse (including rape);

c) Another treatable issue is when the minor seeks therapy for diagnosis or treatment of drug or alcohol related problems and the therapist is a provider under contract with the state or a county to provide alcohol or drug abuse counseling services. Family Code § 6929.

d) Minor may consent to medical care related to the prevention or treatment of pregnancy, except sterilization or abortion. Family Code § 6925.

<u>Record Keeping Under These Circumstances</u>

When treating without parental consent the therapist must state in the minor's records whether or when attempts were made to contact parents or legal guardian and whether such attempts were successful or reasons why such contact would be inappropriate.

There a number of applicable laws regarding the treatment of minors. Family Code § 6924 states that a minor who is 12 years or older may consent to mental health treatment or counseling on an outpatient basis if both of the following requirements are satisfied:

♦ The minor, in the opinion of the attending professional person, is mature enough to participate intelligently in the outpatient services.

♦ The minor would present a danger of serious physical or mental harm to self or to others without the mental health treatment or counseling or is the alleged victims of incest or child abuse.

Family Code § 6929 indicates that a minor who is 12 years of age or older may consent to medical care and counseling relating to the diagnosis and treatment of a drug or alcohol related problem. As used in this section, "counseling" means the provision of counseling services by a provider under contract with the state or a county to provide alcohol or drug abuse counseling services.

The consent of parent, parents or legal guardian shall not be necessary to authorize these services. Mental health treatment or counseling shall include the involvement of minor's parent, parents or legal guardian, unless in the opinion of the professional person who is treating the minor, such involvement would be inappropriate. The therapist shall state in the patient record whether and when (date and time) he or she attempted to contact the parent, parents or legal guardian of the minor, and whether such attempt was successful or unsuccessful, or the reason why, in his or her opinion, it would be inappropriate to contact the parent, parents or legal guardian of the minor.

A noncustodial parent has a right to access his or her child's records. Access to records and information pertaining to a minor child, cannot be denied because the parent is not the child's custodial parent.

Health and Safety Code § 1795.14 indicates "the representative of a minor shall not be entitled to inspect or obtain copies of the minor's patient records under . . . the following circumstances . . . Where the health care provider determines that access to the patient records would have a detrimental effect on the provider's professional relationship with the minor patient or the minor's physical safety or psychological well-being."

Emancipated Minors

Any person under the age of 18 years who comes within the following description is an emancipated minor:

(a) Who has entered into a valid marriage, whether or not such marriage was terminated by dissolution; or

(b) Who is on active duty with any of the Armed Forces of the United States of America (minors 16 and older may enlist); or

(c)   Who has received a declaration of emancipation
from the superior court of the county. A minor must
be at least 14 years old before he or she can
receive such a declaration.

EIGHT

wisdom

Endings

This chapter begins with the guiding principle of wisdom. As noted earlier in chapter one, wisdom is considered a function of spiritual development in Taoist thought and is an extremely valuable quality in the practice of psychology and tends to distinguish effective therapists (Hanna & Ottens, 1995). Wisdom can lead to a full participation in life and work with others. While intelligence is needed to grasp the concepts of an ethical practice, wisdom allows for the appropriate application of standards, guidelines, and theories and assists in the resolution of ethical dilemmas. Ambiguity is also accepted and a comfort with its shades of uncertainty is experienced. As you read the following sections, you may wish to note your level of comfort with some of the more ambiguous elements. The following sections focus on the referral process, referral categories, referring cases out to other practitioners, addressing secrets, and the termination process.

Referrals and Adjunctive Services

In the practice of psychotherapy and in the role of therapist, one is involved in a variety of ongoing assessments, including initially striving to identify the patient's needs and recognizing and acknowledging one's own limitations with regard to those needs. Appropriate referrals are also made with the patient's best interest in mind.

Two major categories of referrals are presented in the following pages and divided into essential and complementary referrals. Additionally, a myriad of commonly used referrals are included to assist you in discerning the specific referral sources needed for your particular case. Hopefully, these will provide you with resources to strengthenr case management ability; assist you in developing case presentations; enhance your ability to respond to vignettes in a comprehensive manner for an oral examination; and provide resources for your future work with patients.

Essential Referrals

These occur in emergencies or crises, such as when medical attention is called for, and in situations where all trained psychotherapists would likely utilize an adjunctive service. Several examples follow;

A potential client presents the psychotherapist with a conflict of interest–the usual ethical course of action is to refer to another therapist; A patient presenting with a possible neurological dysfunction–a medical screening and neuropsychological evaluation would be essential prior to engagement in psychotherapy; A chemically dependent individual or family presenting with these issues– would be referred to available adjunctive services such as 12-step programs (Alcoholics Anonymous, Al-Anon, Al-Ateen, etc.).

Complementary Referrals

This category of referral goes beyond the emergency or crisis situation and is meant to provide an enrichment to the psychotherapeutic process. An example is referring a couple you are working with to a couples communication training group or referring parents to a parenting class such as Systematic Training for Effective parenting or Parent Effectiveness Training.

Commonly Utilized Referrals and Adjuncts

*This is an example of some resources
that may exist within your community.*

Crisis Referrals

- ◆ Emergency Room: Immediate medical or psychiatric assistance. Alternatively, some communities have mobile Psychiatric Assessment Teams.
- ◆ Law Enforcement Agency such as Police or Sheriff's Department: useful when following through with the Tarasoff warning; Child Abuse Report; Protection of the patient or therapist
- ◆ Hotline: Information, Referral and Support for patient or family members
- ◆ Rape Crisis Center: Crisis counseling, Ongoing Counseling, support, family and partner assistance

- Shelter: Safe respite; Shelter for homeless or battered women and children
- Social Services: Child and adult protective services; assistance with money, food, clothing, and shelter. General relief is a service generally designed for the homeless.

Clinically Related Adjunctive Referrals

- Child Psychologist or Child Psychotherapist: Special expertise in working with children
- Clinical Psychologist: Psychological testing
- College or University Counseling Centers: Helpful for patients who are students, often provide low-cost services, such as short-term topical groups
- Group Therapy: Adjunctive or sole treatment
- Neuropsychologist: Neuropsychological evaluation
- Pastoral Counselor or Clergy: Religious or spiritual
- Psychiatrist: Psychopharmacological consultation
- Residential Treatment: Structured and specialized.
- School Guidance Counselor: Guidance in vocational opportunities, future academic development
- Sex Therapist: Sexual dysfunction that you are not qualified to treat
- Vocational Counselor: Occupational testing; Career development and counseling

Legal Resources

- American Civil Liberties Union
- Attorney or Legal Clinic or Legal Assistance Center
- Attorney General's Office
- District Attorney's Office: Generally provides victims and witnesses of crimes with information and resources; information on court hearings or protective orders/restraining orders.

♦ Family Violence Legal Center or Battered Woman's Legal Office: information on restraining orders
♦ Licensing Boards or Professional Associations: To register ethical complaints with board or association
♦ Patients' Rights Advocate: Assists psychiatric patients with information, violation or denial of rights, representation at civil certification review hearings, Social Security Disability Insurance hearings

Educational or Occupational Resources

♦ School Systems: Pupil personnel services and attendance counselors; nurses; Special education services; Services for students with disabilities
♦ Library: Resources for information and research
♦ Child's School: Principal or teacher for school related child and/or family problems
♦ Employment Development Department: Employment services
♦ Social Services: Welfare services, employment assistance, In-home care
♦ Employment agencies: Job recruitment, placement, and training
♦ Employee Assistance Program: Employee services for issues interfering with job satisfaction or productivity.

Medically Related Referrals

♦ Family Physician: Physical exams to rule out organic causes; consult with eating disorder team
♦ Neurologist: To assess and diagnosis organic mental disorders
♦ Veterans Administration (VA) Hospital
♦ Psychiatrist: Consultation and Medication Evaluation
♦ Urologist or Gynecologist
♦ HIV Testing Center; AIDS Projects

- Hospice Care; Skilled Nursing Facility
- Physical Therapy; Bodywork; Massage
- Detoxification Center
- Registered Dietitian

Self-Help and Support Groups

- Coming Out Groups; Gay Men's Groups; Lesbian Groups
- Alcoholics Anonymous (*currently over 150 Anonymous groups*)
- Al Anon; Alateen, Alatot
- CoDA Group: CoDependents Anonymous
- Cocaine or Narcotics Anonymous
- Sex Addicts Anonymous
- Dreamtending or Dream Work Groups
- Adult Children of Alcoholics: ACA groups, ACOA workshops
- Eating Disorder Groups: Overeaters Anonymous; Specifically focused group therapy.
- Survivor Groups such as Incest Survivors: Daughters United, Daughters and Sons United; Incest Survivors Anonymous; Men's survivor groups.
- Survivor Groups (other Traumas): Children of Holocaust Survivors; Plane Crash Survivors; Prisoners of War
- Parents Groups: Parent Effectiveness Training (PET); Systematic Training for Effective Parenting (STEP); Parents United
- Support Groups for Patient's Families
- Smoking Cessation Groups
- Specific Racial or Ethnic or Cultural Support Group
- Singles Groups: Parents Without Partners for single parents; community organizations such as YMCA, YWCA, churches

Referral Process

In contemplating and making referrals, the therapist needs to consider a number of factors, including:

1. Familiarity with the referral source, including the services offered, ethical treatment provided, and quality of services.

2. Which specific person, community agency, or service is best qualified to help the patient.

3. Limitations or constraints that would make it difficult for the patient to gain or benefit, e.g., geographic or physical inaccessibility, unaffordable cost, or language.

4. Whether the therapist should reach out or whether the patient should make the contact with the referral source; or whether a meeting with the referral source, the therapist, and the patient should occur.

5. The patient's readiness and willingness to access the referral.

6. Legal and ethical issues that emerge with a referral–confidentiality being the primary one.

Referring Case Out

It is considered ethical practice to disengage and refer the patient out for therapy when it would be improper for you to be, or continue to be, the psychotherapist in the case. Several situations follow:

• The case is outside your scope of practice or the course of therapy is outside your level of training and experience. Examples of cases outside scope of practice could include a referral for conducting a battery of neuropsychological tests. A referral for conducting a child custody evaluation could be outside your scope of training.

- You have had previous relationships with the potential patient, such as a friendship, or the potential patient is related to you, or is your student.

- Potential patient is in a family, friendship, or intimate relationship with an existing patient causing unresolvable boundary or confidentiality issues.

- You become aware of how countertransference is interfering with your ability to provide effective psychotherapy, and you are unable to address it sufficiently through a range of methods including personal therapy, consultation, or supervision. The best interest of your patient is clearly an active principle here.

- Having obtained peer or other professional consultation, and concluding you are not effectively treating the patient, and are unable to do so, you must refer the patient to a more capable psychotherapist.

BEST TO REFER A CASE OUT WHEN:

Case Is Outside Scope of Practice
Previous Relationship with Patient
Existing Patient Connection-Unresolvable
    Confidentiality or Boundary Issues
Countertransference Interfering With
    Provision of Effective Therapy
Post Consultation & Cannot Resolve
    the Problem

Release of Information

It is essential to obtain an appropriate release (preferably written) before breaching therapist-patient confidentiality. This written release includes the patient's written consent.

Guidelines for release of information:

- Absent an applicable legal* or ethical exception, everything disclosed by a patient to a therapist is considered confidential, including the therapist's thoughts based on such information (e.g., diagnosis), and is not to be disclosed to anyone else.   This includes the fact that the patient is in therapy. *Legal exception: A provider of health care may speak with another licensed person regarding the patient, if purpose is for diagnosis or treatment of the patient (Civil Code § 56).

- A release from confidentiality is one of the exceptions which allows the therapist to divulge otherwise confidential information. The release must be secured from the patient, and it is good practice (although not mandatory) to secure the release from confidentiality in writing.

- Releases are commonly secured from the patient in conjunction with referrals to other helping professionals such as physicians, psychiatrists, or other therapists. They are also routinely obtained when the patient is referred in by someone else such as a probation officer, school counselor, or minister.

- Releases are also commonly utilized by insurance or managed care companies as a prerequisite to payment, so that a representative of the company may speak with the therapist about the treatment issues and related therapeutic actions.

- Even if the patient has given his or her other therapist, physician, or minister permission to talk with you, you still need a release from the patient before you can breach your confidential relationship with the patient, absent another applicable exception.

Secrets–Guidelines in Considering Secrets

As a prudent practice issue, it is suggested that therapists establish reasonable and consistent policies concerning how to handle secrets disclosed to the therapist by a patient in conjoint therapy. Approaches range from never disclosing to always disclosing all content. Whatever your particular policy will be, it is recommended to share this at the outset of treatment as part of obtaining informed consent for treatment. The following are several types of policies and practices:

1. During the initial session, the therapist may describe the basic intention in conjoint treatment: to say and hear everything *in session*, and that the therapist maintains the right to disclose confidential information, if he or she feels it is in the best interest of the patients. Some psychotherapists explain that they assume the holder of a secret wants help in disclosing it, which they will provide. This type of policy may be clarified if one spouse attempts to share a secret.

2. When a secret is disclosed to the therapist privately, he or she reminds the holder of the secret of the policy, and works toward disclosure (by the holder of the secret) in conjoint session. Example: Information regarding an affair or sexual liaison.

   If a patient refuses to reveal the secret:

   a) The therapist assesses whether or not the patient is committed to improving the relationship.
   b) If the patient is committed to improving the relationship, a referral for individual therapy might be advisable, to work through resistance to disclosing. Under this arrangement, conjoint therapy would continue, with the secret held until the disclosure was made.
   c) If the patient is not invested in improving or staying in the relationship, the therapist may use the conjoint session to make this explicit. Concurrently, the therapist may no longer feel effective as a conjoint therapist, and may refer out for further therapy without giving the specific reason (i.e., that patient won't reveal secret).

3. Unusual or unique circumstances may present complex dilemmas for the therapist without an explicit policy. A therapist may choose to hold a secret confidential and continue working with the couple, if in his or her sound clinical judgment, it is in the best interest of the patient. An important question when working with a couple, is "who is the pa-

tient?" Each individual, or the relationship, or all of the above? The answer to this question may prove helpful to you in developing a policy, if you have not considered these issues yet. Reading the literature, consulting with colleagues, and discussing standards of practice in the field will be helpful for you in creating your working policy.

Closure or Termination Process

Closure or termination remains an integral part of the therapeutic process. Termination may evolve organically after the client has experienced a range of personal gains, implemented support systems, resolved conflicts, and integrated new behaviors. While the termination process may consolidate and summarize the treatment process, and provide the client with opportunities for further developmental growth, individuation, and empowerment, it can also restimulate abuse related issues.

The responsibility to engage in a termination process belongs to the therapist and is addressed explicitly within many profession's ethical codes of conduct. Planning a considerable amount of time for termination and closure issues with abuse survivors is preferred to a brief ending. The number of termination focused sessions is highly dependent on the length of the therapeutic relationship and the context of the treatment. If a therapist is working with clients on a time-limited basis, a referral to an appropriate provider would be given, but if the client is in the midst of a crisis at the pre-specified end of therapy, the therapist addresses those needs until the crisis is resolved.

Sensitively welcoming the potential issues associated with this transition includes inviting the range of feelings that may emerge including any restimulated abuse related issues. Although clearly dependent upon the depth of the relationship, the circumstances of the termination, and the amount of time devoted to the termination, grieving the loss of the intimate therapeutic relationship with the therapist may be necessary and expressions of anger at the perceived abandonment may occur. Further opportunities for growth abound during this process within the safety of the therapeutic relationship.

In some circumstances, the client may express a desire to end the therapeutic process either directly or indirectly. The client may explicitly state that she or he is interested in ending therapy-perhaps prematurely in your professional opinion-or the client has reached a point where it would be helpful to terminate and the original agreed upon goals have been reached. In these situations, validate the client's stated desire, invite the patient to express and acknowledge feelings, thoughts, or images about terminating, and work toward an acceptable resolution. The resolution may consist of a vacation or break from therapy, a full termination, or a referral to another practitioner or form of treatment.

Honoring the client's stated desire to end treatment is essential. Since I view the treatment process as a collaboration, I customarily express my support of the client's wish, inquire further into the desire, and share my clinical perspective. I believe in taking breaks from the therapeutic process when time is needed to consolidate gains made. An explicit discussion about the termination may also reveal undisclosed wishes or needs of the clients that were not raised earlier. For this reason it can prove to be highly empowering and may even move the treatment into deeper realms.

Moving toward closure the therapist can effectively address unfinished questions or concerns, including unstated feelings between the patient and therapist, the patient's perception of the therapy process, especially if this hasn't been done throughout the therapeutic process, and evaluation of the positive aspects and possible disappointments concerning the therapeutic process. The termination phase allows the therapist to acknowledge the client's personal growth, summarize gains and successes, identify major "learnings" for both patient and therapist, discuss possible areas for future work, and recommend future therapy alternatives if the client is interested.

Timing of Termination Process

Sufficient amount of time or reasonable amount of time should be provided for termination and closure issues.

The number of termination focused sessions is highly dependent on the length of the therapeutic relationship and the context of the treatment.

1. Therapeutic Response to Patient Concerns

The patient may present with direct or indirect expression of termination issues. For example, the patient may explicitly state that she or he is interested in terminating therapy (perhaps prematurely in your professional opinion), or it becomes clear that the patient has reached a point where it would be helpful to terminate (the original agreed upon goals have been reached and no other goals have been established). It may be helpful to assist the patient in acknowledging and validating his or her feelings, being aware of working towards an acceptable resolution.

2. Approaching Closure

    Address any unfinished questions or business such as:
    Expression of thoughts or feelings that the patient and/or
    therapist could have done more, summarizing patient's
    perception of the therapy process, sharing positive and
    negative thoughts and feelings between patient and thera-
    pist, and evaluation of the positive aspects and possible
    disappointments concerning the therapeutic process.

3. Transitioning

    Acknowledge patient's personal growth, summarize gains
    and successes, identify major "learnings" for both patient
    and therapist, discuss possible areas for future work and
    recommend future therapy alternatives if the patient is in-
    terested.

    The responsibility to engage in a termination process is the
therapist's. Note the following ethical principle: "Prior to termination for whatever reason, except where precluded by the patient's
or client's conduct, the psychologist discusses the patient's or
client's views and needs, provides appropriate pre-termination counseling, suggests alternative service providers as appropriate, and
takes other reasonable steps to facilitate transfer of responsibility
to another provider if the patient or client needs one immediately"
(APA, 1992, standard 4.09c).

NINE

tranquility

Factors Involved in Taking a Case

Tranquility provides us a frame in which to begin the decision making process related to taking a case. The considerations involved require contemplation that is "absent of motion" as a calm body of water appears immediately prior to immersion. The decision to take a case in psychotherapy is dependent upon several factors. For clarity, I will place these factors into two distinct categories: factors about the patient and factors about the psychotherapist. Assessing and evaluating these factors prior to initiating psychotherapy is best, but may not always be possible. At times these factors come into play during the treatment process and should be attended to properly at that time.

Factors about the Patient

The ethical intention is to provide psychotherapy to patients who are willing, legally suitable, capable of relating to the psychotherapeutic process, and are benefiting from the experience. Working with patients who are not is considered unethical. Most therapists begin from the assumption that anyone is a suitable patient for therapy, then rule out legal and ethical exceptions to this. One considers willingness, legal suitability, capacity for psychotherapy, and appreciable benefits from therapy.

Willingness
Does the person want to be in therapy?
Is there a refusal to cooperate in any
meaningful way if court referred?

Legally Suitable
Is the patient legally suitable for psychotherapy in
terms of age? If the patient is a minor who would
like to be seen without parental consent, does he or
she meet the exception (see section on working
with Minors)? If not, have you sought out parental
consent and received assent from the minor?

Capable of Relating to the Process of Psychotherapy
Communication and Capacity is Considered.

Are there any language or communication difficulties? If your primary language is English and the patient's is not, how comprehensive is the patient's understanding of English (and how comprehensive is your understanding of the patient's language, e.g., Spanish, or sign language?) Is the patient best served with a referral or the addition of an interpreter?

Capacity

Is the person gravely disabled and lacking reasonable capacity to understand psychotherapy? Is he or she able to provide informed consent to treatment?

Is the individual under the influence of drugs or alcohol at the time therapy is provided? Although psychotherapists have varying degrees of prohibitive policies or allowances regarding this issue, substantial intoxication may render an individual incapable of providing informed consent to psychotherapeutic treatment.

Perhaps an alternative treatment context should be considered, e.g., inpatient hospitalization, partial hospitalization program, residential treatment facility, alcohol/drug rehabilitation program, or intensive day treatment program.

Benefits from Psychotherapy

Is the patient appreciably benefiting from the therapy after a reasonable time and effort by the therapist?

Factors in Taking a Case
Patient Factors

- willingness
- legally suitable
- capacity
- benefits from psychotherapy

Factors about the Psychotherapist

The intention here is to provide psychotherapy within the scope of practice, training, and experience. Other factors include the appropriate use of clinical judgment and the impact of multiple relationships and countertransference responses.

Scope of Practice
Is the issue or the work within your scope of practice?
If the issue is not legally within the scope of practice
one refers to an appropriate professional.

Scope of Education, Training, or Experience
Is the issue within your scope of education, training,
or experience? Are you substantially skilled in treating this
population, issue, family developmental stage, etc.? If not
are you seeking sufficient adjunctive training, consultation,
or supervision to assist you?

Multiple Relationships

Do you or have you had a previous relationship with this individual, couple, or family? Are you significantly engaged in other relationships which could impair your objectivity or judgment in this case?

Countertransference

In becoming aware of the range of countertransference reactions to a specific case, you discover an inability to manage them sufficiently–even after seeking consultation or supervision–and they interfere with psychotherapy.

Factors in Taking a Case
Therapist Factors

- scope of practice
- scope of education, training, experience
- multiple relationships
- unmanageable countertransference

Vignette Conceptualization

This section is provided for clinicians wishing to conceptualize their potential responsibilities in the beginning stages of psychotherapy. It also serves the purpose of organizing responses for an oral presentation in a testing situation, such as for the oral licensing exam in psychology or marriage and family counseling. Both of these oral licensing exams usually provide a brief clinical vignette, followed by specific questions regarding a clinician's thought process in deciding to take a case, diagnostic impressions, assessments, treatment plans including goals and empirically based interventions for the particular diagnoses, and use of adjunctive services such as referrals, consultation, and supervision. This requires a certain level of comfort and familiarity with the process of thinking in a systematic and logical manner prior to speaking about the issues, as well as a strategy to articulate a comprehensive and accurate response. The following section offers a variety of methods to use in these situations.

Accepting a Case

Whenever we read or hear a brief case vignette, one of the first determinations is whether it is appropriate for us to treat this particular individual, couple, family, or issue, and if it is within the scope of our practice and education, training, and experience. The decision will emerge after a thorough and systematic exploration of the two primary factors, discussed previously as Factors in Taking a Case–patient factors and psychotherapist factors.

First, determine who the patient is, for example, if presented with a family, will you treat all members or the identified patient, or the couple. Next, explore the patient factors, then the therapist factors.

Therapist Factors

This section requires an exploration of the therapist's scope of practice, education, training, professional experience, as well as abilities and limitations in treating this particular client, population, and issue. Any therapist issues and conflicts that could potentially interfere with the therapeutic process need to be addressed. This area is partly addressed by the reflection on countertransferential responses. The most important aspect here is articulating your limitations and knowing when you need to seek consultation or supervision.

If you determine that it is appropriate for you to accept the case based on a preliminary review of these initial items, then move on to the next section, addressing the issue or problem in greater depth.

"Shadow" Mnemonic

A mnemonic may be helpful to organize the extensive information. A mnemonic is in honor of Mnemosyne, the goddess of memory from classical mythology. Mnemonics comes from the Greek term *mnemonikos*, "of memory, mnemon, mindful. Pertaining to, aiding or intended to aid the memory" (Webster's New Riverside, 1984, p. 760). While Mnemosyne assists the therapist in this process of looking deeply, she may also be evoked for the patient, who is drawing on his or her oral history. I believe there is an art to memory, and have created categories with dramatic tones which represent continuums of experience or behavior. Awareness of the continuum within each category, from a less to more serious progression of events, is best to keep in mind when conducting an assessment.

The mnemonic is: S H A D O W, referring to the unseen, the hidden, not easily seen.

S H A D O W

S	Suicide
H	Homicide
A	Abuse
D	Diversity
O	Organicity
W	Whole Person

Suicide

This category focuses on the range of behavior constituting danger to self. Active and immediate considerations involve the assessment of suicidal ideation and intent, including an expressed means and plan, past history of suicide attempts, level of hopelessness, the presence of support systems.

Homicide

This category focuses on danger to others, including the act of making serious threats of harm. This category allows for a sorting out of the clinician's responsibilities to warn an intended victim (Tarasoff duty to warn).

Abuse

Focuses on abuse, such as elder adult abuse, dependent adult abuse, and child abuse. Mandated reporting duties are also addressed here.

Diversity

Focuses on the aspects of diversity which may remain hidden, unless inquired about. For further explication of diversity another mnemonic is waiting in the wings, GRACE'S ODE:

G R A C E' S O D E:

    G——Gender role

    R——Religion

    A——Age

    C——Cultural context

        (including language and environment)

    E——Ethnicity

    SO—Sexual orientation

    D——Developmental factors

        (individual, family life cycle), and

    E——Economic aspects

        (socio-economic and class issues).

Organicity

Pertaining to the body, such as physiological difficulties, neurological problems, substance use, medications, and eating disorders. Be certain to rule out any medical causes or conditions that may be contributing to the overall diagnostic picture.

Whole Person

Evoking a total view of the whole person in his or her humanness and humanity, not as a psychological or mental disorder, but a person within their full context and life situation, seen through a lens which includes their voice, behavior, thoughts, difficulties, strengths, coping capacities, and limitations. When you arrive at this section, go back to diversity to see if there is any issue likely to impact the provision of service, and address this clearly.

Strategies for Approaching Vignettes in Oral Exam or Presentation Contexts

Five Step Process
- 1. Acquisition
     Read the vignette comprehensively
- 2. Anxiety Management
     Active attention to breathing, being fully present in the moment, awareness of others in the room
- 3. Organization
     Use mnemonics. Allow Mnemosyne to guide you.
- 4. Presentation
     Practice with audience/tape
     Assess yourself for structure and style
- 5. Interaction
     Engage with the individuals in the room.

Acquisition

In this first step, one reads slowly, carefully, and thoroughly. Perhaps a second reading will assist you in comprehending the situation. First, obtain an overview of the situation, then look at specifics.

If you find that it's helpful to imagine the patient in front of you, do so. If you are an auditory learner, you may consider requesting permission to read the vignette aloud. You will usually read it once again for the tape recorder.

Organization

Use mnemonics to assist you in remembering information and providing a full response. The SHADOW mnemonic allows you to address any red flag issues that may be present. Red flag issues are issues which are considered priority items that should be addressed immediately early in the work.

There are certain points most skilled clinicians address immediately if they are presented in a vignette. These are often referred to as red flags, e.g., crisis and mandated reporting issues. Whenever addressing these issues, give full responses addressing the relevant legal standard or ethical issue that informs your practice.

One point on confidentiality. Please remember that it is the therapist's responsibility to hold confidential and safeguard information obtained in the therapy session. Deviations occur when they are necessary to avoid clear and imminent danger to the patient or others or when a mandate within the law takes precedence (e.g., Tarasoff duty to warn). One way to think of this is that responsibility for the decision that confidentiality must be breached rests solely on the therapist's judgment that the potential consequences of maintaining confidentiality are more onerous than if confidentiality were to be breached.

Initial Considerations in Taking A Case

"A SHADOW"

A   Accepting a case.
Factors in Taking a case;
patient and psychotherapist factors.
Assess appropriateness for Treatment;
e.g., age of Minor, and outpatient
versus inpatient concerns.

S   Suicide or Dangerousness to Self

H   Homicide or Dangerousness to others

A   Abuse (child, elder, adult, spousal)

D   Diversity Issues: Diversity leads us to
another mnemonic:
      GRACE'S ODE (see sidebar)

O   Organicity; general medical conditions
that may contribute to the focus of
treatment; physiological concerns such
as neurological disorders, drug or alcohol
use and abuse, eating disorders

W   Whole Person

GRACE'S ODE–in honor of the Three Graces in Greek mythology, considered to be the nature goddesses of gratitude.

G	Gender, gender role
R	Religion
A	Age
C	Cultural context, language
E	Ethnicity (address any relevant acculturation issues)
S	Sexual
O	Orientation
D	Developmental Stage, e.g., of life, or family
E	Economic or class context

There are Five Primary Elements in Vignette Response

I. Taking the Case–Accepting the case
II. Who
III. What
IV. How
V. Other

1. Accepting the case
2. Who is the patient?
3. What is the problem or the issue?
   Shadow, Grace's Ode, Clinical Assessment of issues including DSM IV diagnosis and developmental issues if relevant.

4. How will you intervene? Treatment plan, Interventions for issues, Include adjunctive services and referrals

<u>What–What is the problem or issue?</u>
<u>What are the issues? (Assessment)</u>

♦   What questions/issues do I need to discuss with this patient?
♦   What red flag issues are present? State the legal or ethical standards that inform your action.
♦   Are there safety issues that require action or my reporting to authorities?
♦   Clinical assessment of the issue using DSM IV Differential Diagnosis; Integrate the Mental Status Exam here if relevant to the vignette (Appearance, Behavior, Mood, Affect, Thought process and content, Perception, Insight); assess the developmental stage of the individual, couple, or family.

<u>How–How do you intervene?</u>
<u>What is the treatment?</u>

♦   Develop the best treatment plan
♦   Indicate how you will treat the read flags mentioned under issues
♦   Present goals and interventions for the specific problems being treated. Goals are best stated as consensual goals (therapist and patient have agreed to these).
♦   Be sure to stay within your scope of practice and refer to others when necessary for making referrals
♦   Discuss short-term, intermediate, and long term treatment (if you were to work with the patient longer)

Other Issues

Case management issues can be addressed here, such as seeking adjunctive services in the interest of assisting the patient in meeting his or her goals.

- ◆   Are there any legal, ethical, or conflict of interest issues?
- ◆   Do I need to make any referrals to medical, social service, or legal personnel?
- ◆   How about adjunctive help such as self-help groups.
- ◆   Do I need to develop any therapeutic contracts that involve suicide or therapy commitments?
- ◆   What issues need to be discussed with my supervisor or with a consultant?

Presentation Style

Assessment

Structure your responses clearly and logically, for example:
I have a number of initial considerations in working with this case:

> My first consideration is . . .
> Another consideration is . . .

> My primary diagnosis for this case is . . .
> My secondary diagnosis is . . .

State what other information you would need in order to verify your speculations and make an appropriate assessment.

> I have several concerns about this case.
> If this, then . . .

This style focuses on each potential issue that is reasonably anticipated given the information within the vignette. If this is the diagnosis, then I would proceed in this manner. The goals may follow with the interventions that will be used for each assessment area or identified issue.

> Goals-State the short term, intermediate, and long-termgoals, preferably   consensual, co-created, and collaborative goals.

When assessing, these are several discriminating questions to consider, in addition to red flags.

1. Are expected developmental crises present, such as adolescent rebellion, to which parents react abnormally? Is there a normal developmental crisis intensified by other stressors such as divorce, unemployment, illness, etc.?

2. Is the presenting problem new, or does it reflect a chronic situation? Chronic problems may reflect longer term characterological difficulties in individuals (personality disorders or stylistic characteristics). Acute problems may be due to recently occurring psychosocial stressors. An inquiry into precipitating factors is advised.

PART IV

grace

CROSSING THE RIVER
ENTERING THE STREAM

TEN

peace

ABUSE

Part Four begins with the Chinese pictograms for grace and peace. Grace suggests the importance of helping others along the way and a dedication to peace demands a "greater fidelity to the truth" (Merton, 1961, p.125). Crossing the river can be fraught with danger given the hidden obstacles and hardships encountered on the journey. At times, one must enter the stream in order to negotiate these obstacles. This chapter addresses the legal, ethical, and professional issues related to elder adult abuse, dependent adult abuse, and child abuse. The development of reasonble suspicion, indicators of abuse, and memory controversies are all addressed.

Adult Abuse–Dependent Adult and Elder Abuse

All states have mandated reporting requirements for suspected cases of child abuse or neglect. Most states have similar reporting laws for abuse or neglect of the elderly and dependent adult. For example, the California Reporting laws for child abuse and dependent adult and elder abuse are quite similar. Psychotherapists with limited experience in reporting these different types of victimization and those interested in learning more may contact the adult protective services department in their communities, an elder adult care ombudsman, professional associations regarding training in recognizing abuse, and refer to the Welfare and Institutions Code Section 15610.

Recent Version of Reporting Law

The newer version of the Elder/Dependent Adult Abuse Reporting Law became effective on January 1, 1999 in California. This is contained in the Welfare and Institutions Code beginning with Section 15610. Under this new law, therapists are mandated to report certain forms of abuse which were previously considered optional.

Currently, the categories of physical abuse, neglect, abandonment, isolation, and financial abuse (formerly termed fiduciary abuse) require mandated reports. These changes came about after the Governor signed Senate Bill 2199 and Assembly Bill 1780 in September of 1998.

Dependent Adult and Elder Abuse

When a therapist, "in his or her professional capacity, or within the scope of his or her employment, has observed or has knowledge of an incident that reasonably appears to be physical abuse, abandonment, isolation, financial abuse, or neglect, or is told by an elder or dependent adult that he or she has experienced behavior constituting physical abuse, abandonment, isolation, financial abuse, or neglect, or reasonably suspects abuse shall report the known or suspected instance of abuse by telephone immediately or as so as practically possible, and by written report sent within two working days" (Welfare and Institutions Code §15630). The therapist is required to report that abuse to an adult protective agency, often contained within the social services department.

This new standard is similar–but not identical–to the current child abuse reporting duty, in that reasonable suspicion is now included. Previously, abuse fitting within the categories of abandonment, isolation, financial abuse, and neglect was not mandated, since the law required that the incident of abuse was either observed by the therapist, or that the elder told the therapist about the abuse. As an example, with this new law, it is now clear that if a perpetrator tells a mandated reporter, such as a therapist, that he or she physically abused an elder or dependent adult, the therapist is mandated to report.

Mandated Reports

A known or reasonably suspected case of physical abuse (injury inflicted by other than accidental means), abandonment, isolation, financial abuse, or neglect involving a dependent adult or elderly person must be reported. A telephone report must be made immediately or as soon as practically possible followed up by a written report within two working days. Immunity exists for civil and criminal liability for mandated reports.

Dependent Adult and Elder Adult Abuse

Mandated Reports are
Made Immediately
and followed up by written reports
within two working days

Optional Reports

Reports are optional, not mandated, if the therapist reasonably suspects or has knowledge of types of elder or dependent adult abuse that are not mandated, such that his or her emotional well-being is endangered in any way. The law does not specify what these categories of abuse may be.

Dependent Adult

As per Welfare and Institutions Code §15610, a dependent adult is a "Person . . . between 18 and 64 who has physical or mental limitations that restrict his or her ability to carry out normal activities or to protect his or her rights including, but not limited to, persons who have physical or developmental disabilities or whose physical or mental abilities have diminished because of age." Dependent adult includes persons who are between this age range and are admitted as an inpatient to a 24-hour facility, as defined in the Health and Safety Code Sections 1250, 1250.2, and 1250.3.

Elderly Adult

An elderly adult is any individual age 65 or older.

<u>Physical Abuse</u>

Assault, battery, assault with a deadly weapon, unreasonable physical restraint, prolonged or continual deprivation of food or water, or sexual assault. Sexual assault is sexual battery, rape, rape in concert, spousal rape, incest, sodomy, oral copulation or penetration of a genital or anal opening by a foreign object.

The definition of physical abuse encompasses the following: the use of "physical or chemical restraint or psychotropic medication:

a) for punishment;
b) for a period beyond that for which the medication was ordered pursuant to the instructions of a California-licensed physician and surgeon, who is providing medical care to the elder or dependent adult at the time the instructions are given; or
c) for any purpose not authorized by the physician and surgeon " (WIC §15610).

<u>Neglect</u>

This term includes "the negligent failure of any person having the care or custody of an elder or a dependent adult to exercise that degree of care that a reasonable person in a like position would exercise." This includes a failure to assist in personal hygiene, failure to provide for medical care (for physical and mental health needs), and failure to prevent malnutrition or dehydration.

Self-neglect is now reportable under this new law. The bill responsible for this legislation included historical information on the severity of this problem, referring to the 225,000 incidents annually (of elder or dependent adult abuse in California), and highlighted the fact that in more than fifty percent of all incidents, the adult is unable to meet his or her own needs due to frailty, untreated health conditions, mental or emotional problems, or family dysfunctions.

Elder Abuse–Abandonment

Abandonment is defined as desertion or willful forsaking by anyone having care or custody of an elder or dependent adult. An essential element within the definition is the provision that this is considered under the circumstance in which a reasonable person would continue to provide care and custody.

Isolation

Isolation is defined as fitting into four specific categories, however, if a physician providing care for the dependent or elder adult gives these as medical instructions (as part of the medical care) it is not considered reportable:

a) acts intentionally committed to prevent an adult from receiving mail or phone calls,

b) falsely telling a caller or visitor that the adult does not wish to speak or meet with the individual, and this is done to prevent contact with family, friends, or others.

c) false imprisonment

d) physical restraint for the purposes of preventing the adult from meeting with visitors.

Financial Abuse

Financial abuse is the current term and occurs in situations where one or both of the following exist:

a) When a person takes, secretes, or appropriates an elder or dependent adult's money or property, to any wrongful use, or with the intend to defraud, or

b) When a dependent adult or an elder (who would be considered dependent if between the ages of 18 and 64) *requests* a transfer of property or funds and *a third party does not take reasonable steps* to follow through and *acts in bad faith.*

The American Psychiatric Association proposed a limitation on the duty to report elder abuse or dependent adult abuse that currently serves as a safeguard. The therapist is not required to make a report when the elder or dependent adult tells of the abuse, abandonment, isolation, financial abuse, or neglect, and; the therapist is not aware of any independent corroborating evidence, and; the elder or dependent adult has been diagnosed with a mental illness, defect, dementia, or incapacity, and; the therapist reasonably believes that the abuse did not occur. Note: please remember that this does not impose a duty to investigate a known or suspected incident of abuse.

Elder Abuse–Safety Concerns

In addition to the mandated duty to report, safety concerns for this population must be addressed whether the patient is a victim of abuse, neglect, abandonment, or financial abuse. In some instances in order to ameliorate the abuse, difficult and stressful changes in the environment may occur, such as a change in primary caretaker, residential facility, or skilled nursing home with assisted living programs. The skilled clinician is aware of the potential consequences of such changes, including the potential losses the adult may experience.

Capacity or competency assessments made need to be made and perhaps a guardian appointed. As a psychotherapist, working from a team approach with other professionals will assist you in your work with the elderly and dependent adult population. Referrals may include physicians, psychologists, social workers, marriage and family therapists, elderly care ombudspersons, adult protective services, and in-home health care. For this reason it is important to become familiar with the resources and the specialists available within your community.

Child Abuse

Knowledge of legal standards, ethical issues, and family law is essential for psychotherapists working in the area of child abuse. As the statistics on prevalence of childhood abuse have indicated, even professionals working in areas such as inpatient facilities or outpatient clinics will greatly benefit from the knowledge. A variety of professional responsibilities and liabilities are associated with protecting children from abuse and neglect. Psychotherapists have an ethical and legal obligation to report suspected child maltreatment, generally referred to as child abuse. In California, when a practitioner has a reasonable suspicion of child abuse, a telephone report is made immediately or as soon as practically possible, followed by a written report within 36 hours. Every state has statutes categorizing child abuse as a crime, providing definitions for all terms, and establishing punishments.

There are three sources for laws relevant to child abuse and protection: statutes, regulations promulgated by the executive branch of government, and court decisions. For example, Congress passed the Child Abuse Prevention and Treatment Act in 1974. The National Center on Child Abuse and Neglect emerged from this Act. NCCAN publishes manuals to provide guidance to professionals involved in the child protection system and to nurture community collaboration and quality of service delivery. This agency also provides federal funding for research in child abuse including prevention and treatment.

Therapists are required to have a basic understanding of child abuse, including assessment and reporting, and how one develops a reasonable suspicion of child maltreatment. Reasonable suspicion is based on one's education, training, and experience. Once you have a reasonable suspicion you are expected to follow through with the procedure for making an appropriate report.

Given that each state has specific laws pertaining to the family, it is good practice to become informed about your state's laws and to seek advice from an attorney when faced with a legal question. Professional associations including the American Psychological Association and the American Association of Marriage and Family Therapists, provide legal consultation as membership benefits.

The following information paints a broad brush picture for nationwide practitioners in terms of potentially applicable laws, as these are applicable to practice within the state of California. The overview provides the legal standards and definitions you need to become familiar with, offers options for action, includes assessment guidelines, and concludes with immediate interventions. These elements will assist you in formulating your responses to a child abuse disclosure and the proximal events surrounding a child maltreatment report.

The Federal Definition of Child Maltreatment

Child maltreatment is defined as the physical or mental injury, sexual abuse or exploitation, negligent treatment, or maltreatment of a child by a person who is responsible for the child's welfare under circumstances which indicate harm or threatened harm to the child's health or welfare. This definition is drawn from the Federal Child Abuse Prevention and Treatment Act. 42 United States Code 5106g(4). See also, 45 C.F.R. 1340.2(d). By definition child maltreatment includes the acts of child abuse and child neglect. Definitions specific to a particular state will generally be found in one or more of its civil or criminal statutes.

Child Abuse and Neglect Reporting Act

Child abuse is defined as a physical injury that is inflicted by other than accidental means on a child by another person. A child is defined as an individual under the age of 18. Child abuse can result in physical injuries that may include bruises, abrasions, lacerations, cuts, scratches, scars, burns, fractures, bite marks, central nervous system injuries, or life-threatening injuries.

The term "child abuse or neglect" includes sexual abuse, willful cruelty or unjustifiable punishment, unlawful corporal punishment or injury, and abuse or neglect in out-of-home care. Child abuse or neglect does not include a mutual affray between minors, i.e., injuries caused by two children fighting by mutual consent (California Penal Code §11165.6, 2001). The elements of child abuse and neglect are further defined in specific sections of law.

Sexual Abuse

Sexual abuse refers to sexual assault and sexual exploitation. Sexual assault includes the following acts: rape, statutory rape, rape in concert, incest, sodomy, lewd or lascivious acts upon a child, i.e., adult exposing him or herself or masturbating in front of a child; oral copulation, sexual penetration, and child molestation, i.e., fondling sexually.

The specific conduct described as sexual assault includes the following: 1) any penetration, however slight, of the vagina or anal opening of one person by the penis of another person, whether or not there is the emission of semen; 2) any sexual contact between the genitals or anal opening of one and the mouth or tongue of another person; 3) any intrusion by one person into the genitals or anal opening of another person, including the use of any object for this purpose, except that, it does not include acts performed for a valid medical purpose; 4) the intentional touching of the genitals or intimate parts (including the breast, genital area, groin, inner thighs, and buttocks) or the clothing covering them, of a child, or of the perpetrator by a child, for purposes of sexual arousal or gratification, except that, it does not include acts which may reasonably be construed to be normal caretaker responsibilities; interactions with, or demonstrations of affection for, the child; or acts performed for a valid medical purpose; 5) the intentional masturbation of the perpetrator's genitals in the presence of a child.

Sexual exploitation refers to any conduct involving matter depicting a minor engaged in obscene acts, including preparing, selling, or distributing obscene matter, or employing a minor to perform obscene acts. Sexual exploitation also refers to promoting, aiding, assisting, employing, using, persuading, inducing or coercing a child to engage in prostitution, or a live performance involving obscene sexual conduct, or to either pose or model alone or with others for purposes of preparing a film, photograph, negative, slide, drawing, painting, or other pictorial depiction, involving obscene sexual conduct. Individuals who are responsible for the welfare of minors, such as parents, guardians, or foster parents are sexually exploiting children when they knowingly permit or encourage a child to engage in the above mentioned behaviors. Additionally, sexual exploitation refers to any person who depicts a child in, or knowingly develops, duplicates, prints, or exchanges, any film, photograph, videotape, negative, or slide in which a child is engaged in an act of obscene sexual conduct, California Penal Code §11165.1, 2001.

Adults Abused as Minors

In situations where an adult patient discloses sexual or physical abuse in childhood, a report of the abuse is not mandated. An Informal Opinion of the California Attorney General, published February 3, 1987, indicated the intention of the child abuse reporting law was to protect children. In light of this clarification, a therapist would read the reporting law literally, and report abuse in circumstances where a reasonable suspicion exists of *child* abuse. When therapists acquire reasonable suspicion that children are being victimized they are mandated to file a child abuse report.

Child Neglect

Child neglect is defined into severe neglect and general neglect. Overall child neglect refers to the negligent treatment or the maltreatment of a child by a person responsible for the child's welfare under circumstances indicating harm or threatened harm to the child's health or welfare. The term includes both acts and omissions on the part of the responsible party.

Child Neglect–Severe

Severe neglect refers to the negligent failure of a person having the care or custody of a child to protect the child from severe malnutrition or medically diagnosed nonorganic failure to thrive. Severe neglect means those situations of neglect where any person having the care or custody of a child willfully causes or permits the person or health of the child to be placed in a situation such that his or her person or health is endangered, including the intentional failure to provide adequate food, clothing, shelter, or medical care.

Child Neglect–General

General neglect means the negligent failure of a person having the care or custody of a child to provide adequate food, clothing, shelter, medical care, or supervision where no physical injury to the child has occurred. A child receiving treatment by spiritual means or not receiving specified medical treatment for religious reasons, shall not for that reason alone be considered a neglected child. An informed and appropriate medical decision made by parent or guardian after consultation with a physician or physicians who have examined the minor does not constitute neglect, California Penal Code §11165.2.

Willful Cruelty

Willful cruelty or unjustifiable punishment of a child refers to a situation where any person willfully causes or permits any child to suffer, or inflicts thereon, unjustifiable physical pain or mental suffering, or having the care or custody of any child, willfully causes or permits the person or health of the child to be placed in a situation such that his or her person or health is endangered, California Penal

Code §11165.3.

Unlawful Corporal Punishment

Unlawful corporal punishment or injury refers to a situation where any person willfully inflicts upon any child any cruel or inhuman corporal punishment or injury resulting in a traumatic condition. It does not include an amount of force that is reasonable and necessary for a person employed by or engaged in a public school to quell a disturbance threatening physical injury to person or damage to property, for purposes of self-defense, or to obtain possession of weapons or other dangerous objects within the control of the pupil. It also does not include exercise of the degree of physical control authorized by the Education Code, and an injury caused by reasonable and necessary force used by a peace officer acting within the course and scope of his or her employment as a peace officer, California Penal Code §11165.4.

Abuse or Neglect in Out-of-Home Care

Abuse or neglect in out-of-home care includes sexual abuse, neglect, unlawful corporal punishment or injury, or the willful cruelty or unjustifiable punishment of a child, where the person responsible for the child's welfare is a licensee, administrator, or employee of any facility licensed to care for children, or an administrator or employee of a public or private school or other institution or agency. Abuse or neglect in out-of-home care does not include an injury caused by reasonable and necessary force used by a peace officer acting within the course and scope of his or her employment as a peace officer, California Penal Code §11165.5.

Minor Engaging in Sexual Relations

If the minor is engaging in a sexual relationship and is under the age of 14, a report is required unless the minor's partner is also under 14 and the partner is of similar age. An example here is two 13 year olds engaging sexually. With disparate age differences a report is required. If the minor is 14 or over, a report is not mandated, assuming no coercion is involved and the circumstances of the sexual involvement do not meet other reporting criteria. The following additional criteria require a report: 1) any person who is 21 years of age or older who engages in an act of sexual intercourse with a minor under the age of 16, and 2) any person who is at least 10 years older than the child who is 14 or 15 years old and commits lewd and lascivious acts. As previously mentioned lewd and lascivious is generally defined and interpreted by the courts as causing any touching of a child by the perpetrator or by the child at the direction of the perpetrator for the purpose of arousing, appealing to or gratifying the lust, passions, or the sexual desires of the person or the child. This conduct has been reportable for many years, but was expanded recently to include 14 and 15 year olds.

The following explanatory note refers to minors over 14 engaging in voluntary sexual relationships. This California Court of Appeals ruling held that "a fundamental part of the [child abuse] reporting law is to allow the trained professional to distinguish an abusive and non-abusive situation. Instead of a blanket reporting requirement of all activity of those under a certain age, the professional can make a judgment as to whether the minor is having voluntary relations or being abused" Planned Parenthood Affiliates v. Van de Kamp (181 Cal. App. 3d 245). Regarding minors under 14, the appellate court indicated their provisions contemplated criminal acts of child abuse causing trauma to the victim, and did not contemplate the voluntary sexual associations between young children under the age of 14 who are not victims of a child abuser and are not the subjects of sexual victimization.

Reporting Responsibilities for Child Abuse

Psychotherapists have ethical and legal obligations to report suspected child maltreatment, generally referred to as Child Abuse. In coursework required by professional licensing boards, one learns in depth how a reasonable suspicion of child maltreatment is developed. Reasonable suspicion is based on one's education, training and experience. Reasonable suspicion means that it is objectively reasonable for a person to entertain such a suspicion, based upon facts that could cause a reasonable person in a like position, drawing on his or her training and experience, to suspect child abuse or neglect. The pregnancy of a minor does not, in and of itself, constitute the basis of reasonable suspicion of sexual abuse. Once a professional has reasonable suspicion, it is important to know the procedure for making an appropriate report.

Mandated Reporters

Many professionals are legally mandated reporters of child abuse and neglect. The following list is a sampling of the individuals designated as mandated reporters: teachers, instructional aides, classified employees of public schools, certificated pupil personnel employees of public and private schools, administrators and employees of youth centers or recreation programs, employees of child day care facilities, headstart teachers, foster parents, group home personnel, personnel of residential care facilities, social workers, probation officers, parole officers, employees of school district police or security departments, administrators and counselors in child abuse prevention programs in public and private schools, coroners, medical examiners, investigators for the district attorney's office, family support officers, peace officers, commercial film and photographic print processors, firefighters, animal control officers, members of the clergy, psychologists, social workers, marriage and family therapists, licensed nurses, dentists, dental hygienists, paramedics, optometrists, physicians, child visitation monitors, and employees of police, sheriff's, probation, and welfare departments.

Members of the clergy, such as priests, ministers, rabbis, and other religious practitioners, are also mandated reporters. However, if knowledge or a reasonable suspicion of child abuse or neglect is acquired during a penitential communication such as confession, the clergy member is not subject to the mandating reporting requirement.

Mandated Reporter Training

All mandated reporters are expected to undergo training in child abuse identification and reporting but the law does not excuse mandated reporters from their duty to report if they have not taken the training. Mandated reporters in California are required to make reports to agencies designated by each county. These agencies include police departments, sheriff's departments, county probation departments, and county welfare departments.

California Child Abuse Reporting Law

The following directive is integrated into California law: A mandated reporter shall make a report to an agency whenever the mandated reporter, in his or her professional capacity or within the scope of his or her employment, has knowledge of or observes a child whom the mandated reporter knows or reasonably suspects has been the victim of child abuse or neglect. The mandated reporter shall make a report to the agency immediately or as soon as is practically possible by telephone, and the mandated reporter shall prepare and send a written report thereof within 36 hours of receiving the information concerning the incident. Mandated reporters are required to follow through on the reporting requirement even if the child has expired, regardless of whether or not the possible abuse was a factor contributing to the death, and even if suspected child abuse was discovered during an autopsy, California Penal Code § 11166.

Reporting Responsibility An Individual Duty

The reporting responsibility is considered an individual's duty and cannot be passed on to another colleague, supervisor, or administrator. The only circumstance permitting another individual to follow through on the reporting requirement centers around two or more persons jointly having knowledge of a known or suspected instance of child abuse or neglect. In this case a single report is made after a mutual agreement is reached as to who will make the telephone and written report.

Mandated
Reporting
Is An
Individual
Responsibility

Immunity

The mandated reporter is provided with absolute immunity from criminal and civil liability for reporting as required or authorized by the law and can receive monies for reimbursement of attorney's fees necessary to defend against a civil action brought on the basis of the report. The absolute immunity is provided to professionals for conduct giving rise to the obligation to report, including the collection of data, observation, examination, or treatment of the victim or perpetrator of child abuse. The immunity is applicable for the conduct performed in a professional capacity or within the scope of employment. In enacting the Child Abuse Reporting Act and the many associated amendments throughout the years, the legislature has prioritized the protection given to children by encouraging reports over the potential harm to innocent parties caused by child abuse investigations.

Mandated Reporting Obligations

It is essential to meet any reporting obligations–by phone immediately or as soon as practically possible and in writing within 36 hours–if a professional acquires a reasonable suspicion of child abuse in one's professional capacity. Therapists are not obligated to tell their patients of the report, but it is usually in the best interests of patients and the therapeutic relationship if this information is not withheld. In fact, informing the patient may be essential in order to preserve the therapeutic relationship. A therapist would use appropriate clinical judgment in discerning how to address this and may need to adjust the treatment plan to incorporate the issues that arise from the act of reporting of the abuse. In some instances, a referral to another therapist may be needed if the therapeutic relationship is irreparably damaged.

Child Abuse Reports
are made to
"Designated Agencies"

Child abuse and neglect reports are made to the agencies legally designated by the county to receive reports of child abuse and neglect: any police department, sheriff's department, county probation department if designated by the county, or the county welfare department. These agencies are required to accept reports from mandated reporters and other persons. At times the agency you make the report to lacks the jurisdiction to investigate, for example, in cases where you are practicing in one county and the reported abuse or neglect is occurring in another county or state. Due to 2001 amendments in the Child Abuse and Neglect Reporting Act in California, the agency is now required to immediately refer the case to the proper geographic jurisdiction for the investigation.

Most social service or welfare departments have specific child protective services units that employ trained professionals, often licensed social workers and family therapists, who take these initial reports. Typically, the report is assigned to another individual in order to conduct the investigation.

As stated earlier, a phone report is made immediately. The phone report of a known or suspected instance of child abuse includes your name, business location, and telephone number; the child's name, address, and present location; child's school, grade, and class, if applicable; names, addresses, and telephone numbers of the child's parents or guardians; the nature and extent of the injury; any information that led you to suspect child abuse; and the name, address, telephone, and other relevant information about the person or persons suspected of abusing or neglecting the child. Even if all of this information is not known to the mandated reporter, making a report is still required.

The written reports are submitted on forms adopted by the Department of Justice, *Suspected Child Abuse Report.* In addition to the information indicated above, the written report includes a place for a narrative description, a summary of what the abused child or person accompanying the child said, and information on any known history of similar incidents for the child. The identity of the mandated reporter and the contents of the report are legally confidential, disclosable only to child protective agencies, designated counsel, by court order, or when the mandated reporter has waived confidentiality.

Disclosure of Abuse

A *disclosure* of abuse or neglect is generally defined as revelation of the abusive experience by a child, intentionally or accidentally. Some professionals define disclosure as a discrete event in which the child makes a clear and direct statement about the abuse (Bradley & Wood, 1996; Ceci & Bruck, 1995), while others see disclosure as a process that unfolds incrementally and may involve denial or recantation (Berliner & Conte, 1990; Sorenson & Snow, 1991; Summit, 1983). Disclosures of child abuse and neglect occur in many ways and may be direct, indirect, complete, or partial. Children may begin talking directly and specifically about what has occurred, although this is usually a function of their age, language ability, developmental level, specific circumstances of the abuse, the level of posttraumatic stress, the severity of abuse, their perceived safety, and the context of the therapeutic setting. Disclosures may be more difficult to make for child victims who are sexually abused within the family over long periods of time, do not perceive support from the nonoffending parent, and have experienced severe forms of abuse (Faller, 1989; Sauzier, 1989). Adolescent boys who are approaching puberty may be less willing to disclose sexual abuse due to the awareness of the stigma associated with homosexuality (Urquiza & Keating, 1990; Watkins & Bentovim, 1992). Maternal support has been found to be positively associated with disclosure (Everson, Hunter, Runyan, Edelsohn, & Coulter, 1989; Lawson & Chaffin, 1992) in child sexual abuse.

When disclosure is an incremental process unfolding over time, children may initiate revelations about the abuse by indirectly asking questions about the abusive behaviors in order to understand what has happened or to inquire into the therapist's response. Children may talk in terms that are vague or abstract, they may not have the vocabulary for communicating about the abuse specifically sexual abuse, may feel shame and embarrassment, have promised not to tell, or have been coerced or threatened with further harm, loss, or death if they disclosed the abuse.

Sorenson and Snow (1991) identified a four phase model of disclosure that seeks to explain this incremental disclosure process: denial, disclosure which may be tentative or active, recantation, and reaffirmation. A child victim's ability to verbally disclose experiences varied over time and was a function of external circumstances such as family pressure and coercion-which also contributed to recantation. Over 92% of the children eventually reaffirmed their allegations in this analysis of common elements of disclosure in 630 cases. Given the prevalent inappropriate reactions to a disclosure of child abuse such as disbelief, blaming, or minimizing, recantation has been considered a common phenomenon (Conte & Berliner, 1981; Rieser, 1991) and is also a risk factor for revictimization (Marx, 1996).

Developing Reasonable Suspicion

When it is objectively reasonable for an individual to entertain a suspicion of abuse based on one's education, training, and experience, *reasonable suspicion* is formed. The process involved in the development of reasonable suspicion is usually derived from the presence of multiple factors and the interpretation of these factors. The factors include observations of physical signs, behaviors, and emotional indicators. Physical marks on a child's body may be prominent, unusual behaviors may be present, explicit statements or disclosures may be made, emotional and psychological symptoms may appear, and parent-child interactions may yield information about familial interpersonal dynamics.

The following categories and indicators will assist in the process of formulating reasonable suspicion. Although the indicators are correlated with child maltreatment, they may or may not be indicative of child abuse or neglect in the specific instance you are assessing. At the absolute minimum, your professional curiosity will be engaged leading you to inquire and seek more information about the circumstances. However, mandated reporters do not engage in investigations of child maltreatment-they merely make the reports once reasonable suspicion is attained.

Becoming familiar with the literature on child maltreatment assists in the process of understanding the indicators of child abuse and neglect. Consultations with child protection service workers, attorneys, clinical supervisors, and professional associations are also good sources to rely on when experiencing confusion or difficulty when assessing potential indicators of child maltreatment.

Parental Clues to Assess for Child Maltreatment

A body of extensive literature exists on parental or perpetrator characteristics (Milner, 1991; Milner & Chilamkurti, 1991). One significant finding indicates that although a percentage of abused children become abusive parents, estimated at 30%, (Kaufman & Zigler, 1987), most of them do not become abusers (Widom, 1989). When an intergenerational history of child abuse or neglect exists, it functions as an important but not conclusive aspect in developing reasonable suspicion of child maltreatment.

Many of these parental and perpetrator characteristics reflect high levels of distress or dysfunction and inappropriate parenting strategies (Factor & Wolfe, 1990). Behaviorally parents have been found to exhibit inconsistent child-rearing practices that reflect critical, hostile, or aggressive styles (Trickett & Kuczynski, 1986). Cognitively abusive parents tend to hold negative attributions toward their children's behavior or tend to perceive their children in negative ways (Azar & Siegel, 1990). Abusive parents may exhibit little attention to their children or express limited positive affect and behavior toward them (Caliso & Milner, 1992; Kavanaugh, Youngblood, Reid, & Fagot, 1988).

Basic parental clues to assess for abuse: Parent may scapegoat the child; may be unable to describe positive characteristics of child; may have unrealistic expectations of the child, e.g., toilet-training a 6 month-old child; may be unduly harsh and rigid about child rearing practices; may turn to child to have his or her own needs met. If the parental explanation for the child abuse injury or symptom does not fit the injury, concern should be heightened.

Parental Clues to Assess for Child Maltreatment

- Parent may be unable to describe positive characteristics of child;

- Perceives child in negative manner;

- Appears unconcerned about child's injuries or minimizes them;

- Limited attention expressed to the child;

- Inappropriate parenting strategies, e.g., rigid style or harsh discipline inappropriate to the child's age or misbehavior;

- Critical, hostile, or aggressive style of parenting;

- Unrealistic expectations of the child, e.g., toilet-training a six month-old child;

- May turn to child to have his or her own needs met;

- Parental explanation for the child abuse injury or symptom clearly does not fit the injury;

- Exhibits high level of psychological distress or behavioral dysfunction.

Indices of Emotional Maltreatment

Emotional maltreatment encompasses an injury to the intellectual or psychological capacity of the child. This is evidenced by observable and substantial impairment or deterioration in the child's ability to develop and function. Thus the socialization process is central in understanding emotional maltreatment and its impact. Emotional maltreatment exists in acts of commission and omission: when a parent or caregiver fails to provide for the appropriate emotional development of the child, intentionally inflicts mental suffering, or permits endangerment of the child. This type of maltreatment rarely constitutes one acute episode and is more often persistent, ongoing, and chronic within predictable and pervasive patterns (Hart & Brassard, 1994). It also coexists with other forms of neglect or abuse.

Emotional maltreatment remains a unique child abuse category, in that it irregularly constitutes a mandated report. This is due to the variability between states: some jurisdictions permit reporting, other states mandate it, while others mandate specific subcategories such as willful cruelty. The infliction of willful cruelty is the only subcategory of emotional maltreatment that currently mandates a child abuse report in California. This constitutes behavior that willfully causes or permits any child to suffer, inflicts unjustifiable physical pain or mental suffering, or having the care or custody of any child, willfully causes or permits the person or health of the child to be placed in a situation such that his or her person or health is endangered. In attempts to clarify child abuse and neglect reporting requirements within California, the permissible section including the terms "may report" was inadvertently removed from the law. This allowed professionals to make reports when they had a reasonable suspicion of emotional maltreatment. Many anticipate the reintegration of this section into the Child Abuse and Neglect Reporting Act by 2002 or soon thereafter.

Emotional maltreatment has been the most controversial and at times ambiguous category of abuse. Advances have been made in understanding the developmental consequences of certain parental behaviors. An early framework proposed emotional maltreatment as an impairment to the child's competence in the world, such as the ability to communicate and acquire patience. In light of this competence model four principles were developed to define the dangers to a child's developing competence. The first two were seen as threats to a child's infancy while the latter are threats to childhood and adolescence: 1) the punishment of a range of childhood positive behaviors including smiling, mobility, exploration, vocalization, and manipulation of objects in the environment; 2) discouraging caregiver-infant bonding; 3) punishment of self esteem; and 4) punishing interpersonal skills necessary for adequate performance in society (Garbarino, 1978).

Emotional maltreatment includes a range of parental or caregiver behaviors: verbal and emotional assault, isolation or close confinement of the child, extreme inattention to the child's needs for attention, affection, or emotional support, and the encouragement of severe maladaptive behaviors. Research-supported subtypes of psychological maltreatment were proposed in the last decade: spurning, terrorizing, isolating, exploiting, corrupting, and denying emotional responsiveness (Hart & Brassard, 1994). Emotional maltreatment may be revealed through specific parental behaviors including: blaming, ridiculing, denigrating, publicly humiliating, scapegoating the child, or other overtly hostile behaviors; demanding excessive responsibility, demanding responsibility inappropriate for the child's developmental level, or setting other rigid expectations; treating children in the family unequally, singling out a child consistently to criticize or punish; and may use fear-inducing, threatening, or violent behaviors toward the child or child's loved objects or pets.

Some behavioral indicators of child emotional maltreatment parallel other categories of abuse. The child may not seek comfort when distressed (Crittenden & Ainsworth, 1989); engages in frequent self-denigrating comments; behavioral problems are noticed in school, such as aggression or disruptions (Hart & Brassard, 1991); evidence of social withdrawal, isolation, feelings of inadequacy and unworthiness (Burnett, 1993; O'Hagan, 1993), reduced emotional responsiveness, low self-esteem, and negative self-concept are evident (Rohner & Rohner, 1980; Shengold, 1989).

Child's Behavioral Indicators
of Emotional Abuse

- The child may not seek comfort when distressed;

- Expresses self-denigrating comments;

- Exhibits behavioral problems (aggressive or disruptive);

- Demonstrates reduced emotional responsiveness;

- Displays extreme behaviors including aggression and hostility;

- Becomes self-destructive, withdrawn or suicidal;

- Somatic complaints including sleep disturbances;

- May exhibit low self-esteem or negative self-concept.

The emotionally maltreated child may display similar signs of emotionally disturbed children, so it is essential to look to the parent's attitudes and behaviors, the societal and cultural context, and the child's developmental mastery of tasks, including attachment during infancy (Bowlby, 1980), development of symbolic representation during toddler ages, development of self-control, gender identity and social relationships during preschool, moral reasoning and peer relationships during latency age, and renegotiation of family roles during adolescence (Hart & Brassard, 1994). If developmental or other disorders are suspected, a referral for psychological testing is pertinent.

Child behaviors are very important elements in assessing emotional maltreatment, but they should not be used as the sole basis for determining maltreatment. Neither does the absence of symptomatic behavior rule out abuse, since the behavioral or psychological impact may be significantly delayed. The intensity, frequency, chronicity, and pervasiveness of the acts along with the impact on the child should all be considered when initially assessing emotional maltreatment.

Physical Abuse

Physical abuse is generally used to describe any non-accidental (intentional) physical injury to a child caused by the child's parent or other caretaker. The range of physical indicators includes bruises, burns, bites, cuts, and fractures. These indicators may range from minor to severe manifestations and some may not definitively indicate physical abuse. For example, bite marks may indicate a deliberate form of physical abuse by a caretaker, an aggressive injury perpetrated by another child, a neglected or poorly supervised child bitten by an animal, or self-injurious behavior. Bruises may develop from play, but located on certain parts of the body may indicate abuse, such as the back of the legs or on the genitals. Other physical indicators are more likely manifestations of abuse including cigarette burns in unusual places, especially on the soles of the feet, palms of the hands, the abdomen, and the buttocks.

Burns resembling sock-like or glove-like markings on the hands or feet, or doughnut-like burns on the buttocks or genital area may be seen. These burns are caused by forced immersion in scalding liquids or extremely hot water. Appliance or tool burns such as fireplace pokers and irons, may leave an imprint on the child's body. A belt buckle print, palm print, or imprint around the torso would suggest the child had been hit with a rope, belt, or cord (Davis, 1982). Intentional infliction of abuse is often suspected in the presence of rope burns on the arms, legs, neck, or torso. Multiple fractures, spiral fractures, and dislocations may indicate repeated physical abuse (Faller, 1981). Severe shaking, or shaken baby syndrome, can lead to a myriad of neurological problems, acute symptoms consisting of vomiting, seizures, or brain swelling, retinal detachment, and hemorrhage (Crime and Violence Prevention Center, 2000). Abdominal injuries may occur from severe blows, kicks, or incidents of deceleration, where a child is thrown against a wall. These injuries may involve the spleen, intestines, liver, kidney, bladder, or pancreas.

In all instances when physical indicators are unexplained or unreasonable explanations are given, preliminary suspicions about maltreatment should be developing. One begins to assess additional characteristics.

Behavioral Indices of Child Physical Abuse

The behavioral indices should serve as warning signs to look further. The information on child behavioral indicators and symptoms is derived in large part from literature involving clinical samples, unlike adult samples where studies were conducted with both clinical and nonclinical samples for comparison. Child behaviors are very important elements in assessing child abuse, however they should not be used as the sole basis for determining abuse. Conversely, the absence of symptomatic behavior would not rule out abuse, since developmental impacts on child behavior may be delayed or hidden. The behaviors may also represent responses to other traumas or mental disorders.

Child Physical Abuse Indicators

- BRUISES–located on the face, lips, torso, back, or buttocks;

- BURNS–cigarette burns, rope burns, appliance burns, and scalding liquid burns;

- FRACTURES–Fractures to the skull, nose, or facial structure– in different stages of healing;

- SWOLLEN LIMBS–Swollen or tender limbs;

- LACERATIONS–Lacerations and abrasions to the mouth, lips, gums, eyes, backs of arms, external genitalia, legs, or torso;

- ABDOMINAL INJURIES–including swelling and localized tenderness, constant vomiting;

- BITE MARKS–human adult or animal bite marks.

Munchausen Syndrome by Proxy Abuse

Munchausen syndrome by proxy is an insidious form of physical abuse that can result in severe physical and psychological impairment, disfigurement, unnecessary and painful medical procedures, and death: a healthy child is placed under repeated medical scrutiny by a caretaker, often the mother, who fabricates the signs and symptoms of illness. This fabrication is deliberate and involves covert or overt acts such as suffocation, administration of inappropriate or excessive medications such as insulin, ipecac syrup, or laxatives (Hughes & Corbo-Richert, 1999), arsenic poisoning, placing foreign fluids such as urine or blood into fluid samples, the use of bacteria or feces placed in feeding tubes, intravenous line contamination in hospital settings (Fulton, 2000), creating the appearance of an injury with menstrual or animal blood, or the actual cutting or injury of the child.

Physical Abuse Behavioral Indices

- Child exhibits sudden changes in behavior or mood, e.g., extreme fear or withdrawn behavior around others, overly compliant, indiscriminate attachments, or changes in behavior with peers;

- Inability to establish good peer relations, aggressive behavior;

- Child may become hypervigilant, watchful, depressed, or underactive;

- May become accident prone or engage in self injurious behavior;

- Regressive behaviors;

- Child is unable to manage his or her behavior resulting in rages, panic, or agitation.

This type of physical abuse is very difficult to assess for the caretaker's behaviors typically appear to be within a normal range of caring and the targeted child is often an infant or toddler. Parent child enmeshment often exists but may be perceived as warranted given the physical disorders. Although the prevalence of Munchausen syndrome by proxy is not known, it is considered to be a rare form of child physical abuse (Helfer, Kempe, & Krugman, 2000).

Neglect

Neglect is defined as a parent's or other caregiver's inattention to the child's basic needs. Neglect includes: abandonment, lack of supervision, nutritional neglect, medical/dental neglect, inappropriate/insufficient clothing, hygiene neglect, shelter neglect, educational neglect, and the failure to thrive syndrome. A child who has been physically neglected may show observable signs of gross malnourishment, failure to thrive, or developmental delays (Crittenden & Ainsworth, 1989) but most types of neglect leave no physical marks. Behaviorally the child may engage in avoidant behavior, may isolate self, or interact less with peers than other non-neglected children (Hoffman-Plotkin & Twentyman, 1984). The child may be depressed, passive, or may seem uninterested in soliciting care and warmth from caretakers or teachers. However powerful these descriptors are, none of the examples convey the utter hopelessness of a neglected child's life.

Neglect is more frequently reported among younger children with reports declining as children get older, although neglect has also been found among adolescents. Furthermore, infants are more likely to be neglected. Neglect may exist when a caregiver fails to provide for adequate physical health care, mental health care, education, supervision, nutrition, household sanitation, or personal hygiene

Behavioral Indicators of Neglect

- Gross malnourishment;
- Chronic hunger;
- Developmental delays;
- Avoidant behavior;
- Child may Isolate self;
- Interacts less with peers;
- Depressed mood or passive behavior;
- Uninterested in soliciting care or warmth;
- Nonorganic failure to thrive.

Physical Indicators of Neglect

- Poor hygiene evidenced by torn or dirty clothing, or inadequate garments for the weather conditions;

- Lack of supervision in especially dangerous situations or activities over long periods of time

Various causes of neglect have been hypothesized including the economic, societal, and personalistic theories. While economic variables such as poverty do play a significant part in many cases of neglect, this does not account for most of the neglect.

Weissbourd (1996) reported that African-American children were nearly three times more likely than white children to be poor. In that same year the Children's Defense Fund (1996) found 58% of abused and neglected children were white, 27% were African-American, and 10% were Hispanic. Societal theories of neglect attribute this form of maltreatment to the institutions and societal values that support it such as reductions in public assistance, welfare, and aid for dependent children. Personalistic theories attribute neglect to individual parental personalities and character structures (Polansky, Chalmers, Buttenwieser, & Williams, 1991). Cantwell (1980) attributed neglectful parenting to "lack of knowledge, lack of judgment, and lack of motivation" (p.184). Some parental indicators involve low motivation, feelings of apathy or futility, and chaos within the home. Neglect as a phenomenon may involve the interaction of all of these variables.

Nonorganic failure to thrive is a subcategory within neglect and refers to more than lack of nutrition. If understimulated, children experience impairments in psychomotor development and may not crawl, stand, or roll over at the developmentally appropriate times. For example, an eighteen month old child should know how to grasp and would request contact with the parents or caretakers. Children who are failing to thrive may be seriously ill and in danger of dying. Faller (1981) theorized infants sense the distancing feelings or disengaged attitudes of their parents and react negatively, showing little interest in food, and turning inward. Indicators of failure to thrive may present in a child who appears overly self-directed, does not look for adult contact, exhibits hoarding or gorging feeding behaviors, and engages in indiscriminate attachments.

Sexual Abuse

Sexual abuse includes any contacts or interactions between a child and an adult in which the child is being used for the sexual stimulation or gratification of the perpetrator or other person. Sexual abuse may also be committed by a person under the age of 18 when that person is either significantly older than the victim or when the perpetrator is in a position of power or control over another child. Examples include: genital fondling, molestation, exhibitionism, rape, pedophilia, incest, or other sexual exploitation such as child pornography or prostitution.

Sudden changes in behavior often serve as red flags that something of concern has occurred. Behavioral changes can function as indicators of distress at home, school, or among peers. The behavioral manifestations may also indicate the onset of a coercive relationship or the occurrence of a traumatic incident. Sudden change may manifest as a regressive behavior, a withdrawing or attention drawing behavior, or in physiological symptomatology.

A range of consequent behaviors may result from the sexual abuse. Children exhibit increased sexual behavior (Friedrich, Grambsch, Broughton, Kuiper, & Beilke, 1991; Gil & Johnson, 1993); may exhibit suicidal behavior (Lanktree, Briere, & Zaidi, 1991) may develop eating disorders; alcohol or other substance abuse problems (Singer, Petchers, & Hussey, 1989); may run away or be truant (Hibbard, Ingersoll, & Orr, 1990); may exhibit fear, anxiety, and concentration problems (Conte & Schuerman, 1987); engage in self injurious behaviors, such as cutting, burning, pulling out hair (van der Kolk, Perry, & Herman, 1991).

Children's interests in sexuality should raise concerns in some situations and may be indicators of prior experiential knowledge gained from abusive or coercive relationships. When an interest in sexuality or compulsive sexual activities dominates other interests that are developmentally appropriate for the child's age, such as playing with schoolmates, concerns often arise about a child's behavior. The overt sexualized behavior described as sequela to sexual abuse is more characteristic with children from age two to six (Friedrich et al., 1992). Children are naturally curious about sexuality and these interests are usually balanced with other explorations within their lives.

Concerns may emerge when children exhibit more sophisticated sexual knowledge than peers coming from similar cultural or familial backgrounds. School aged children tend to engage in sexual explorations with other children their age, but concerns would arise when they engage in sexual behaviors with children much older or younger, when other children repeatedly raise concerns about another child's sexual behaviors, particularly situations where children utilize bribes, coercion, or physical force, and any situations that involve oral or genital contact with animals.

Behavioral Indicators - Sexual Abuse

- Sudden changes in behavior, clinging, regressive, withdrawal;

- Sleep disturbances;

- Increased sexual behavior;

- Alcohol or other substance abuse;

- Poor peer relationships;

- Truancy, delinquency, running away;

- Fear, Anxiety, Concentration problems;

- Expressions of discomfort, pain, or itching in the genital or rectal areas

- Unusual sexual knowledge for developmental level;

- Self injurious behaviors;

- Suicidal feelings or behavior

Memory Controversies That Inform Clinical Practice

Memory becomes central to those who have been required to renounce their perceptions in order to remain safe, survive, or avoid danger. This is true for trauma survivors including children who have experienced the helplessness of ongoing fear and numbness from emotional, physical, and sexual abuse. In Taylor's (1997) study of the military dictatorship in Argentina she categorized this damaging and dehumanizing type of renunciation as *percepticide*. Percepticide "blinds, maims, kills through the senses" (p.124). In cases of child abuse, whether one is the victim, offender, or witness, coming to know the truth, acknowledging what has occurred, no longer denying or avoiding, and transforming the numbness becomes a challenge in the healing process. Percepticide is also a societal practice that must be transformed and overcome in order to prevent abuse, neglect, and other forms of violence.

Issues relating to memory have been hotly contested in clinical, academic (Berliner & Loftus, 1992; Enns, McNeilly, Corkery, & Gilbert, 1995), and legal circles and received sensational media coverage during the 1990's (Jarof, 1993; Safran, 1993). The escalation of conflict between professionals is largely unprecedented although it evokes images of the debates that ensued at the turn of the last century when Freud publicized his patients' reports of sexual abuse. Writings on repressed memory, false memories (Loftus & Ketcham, 1994), delayed memory, memory retrieval, and lawsuits against therapists accused of implanting memories (Pope & Caudill, 2000) have appeared. Psychologists have also been sued by third parties, individuals accused of abuse by the therapist's patients.

The context of these debates is compassionately addressed in an article regarding the cultural backlash against professionals engaged in raising societal awareness about child abuse, specifically sexual abuse (Enns, 1996). The author analyzed the development of this backlash and its function in shifting the focus from the continuing realities of oppression, childhood abuse, and violence. Wylie (1993) noted that our societal reaction to terrible news is instinctually denial or dissociation "societies dissociate their knowledge of trauma—massive injuries, torture, genocide—preferring to live in the 'bleached present' of conventional disbelief and logical denial" (p.43).

Much of this debate has been credited with the clarity developing around standards of practice, given the professional consensus that childhood abuse and traumatic response impact the memory process (American Psychological Association, 1995). For example, caution is recommended when using hypnosis to address memories, audiotaping or videotaping sessions dealing with memory retrieval is advised, and accurate record keeping is suggested. Therapists are advised to become intimately aware of their own biases and begin to understand potential legal vulnerabilities in the therapeutic process.

In terms of competent and ethical practice becoming familiar with the literature is essential. Myers (1989, 1992) offered extensive recommendations for professionals serving as expert witnesses in child sexual abuse litigation, Melton and Limber (1989) addressed the numerous pitfalls in forming professional opinions on memory processes when relying on non-empirical data, Pope (1996) addressed the scientific research on recovered memory, and Pope and Brown (1996) wrote a comprehensive text on the forensic and clinical aspects of recovered memory.

Of significance is the research on traumatic amnesias and the uniqueness of traumatic memories (van der Kolk, Blitz, Burr, & Hartmann, 1984). Traumatic memories may be encoded differently than memories of ordinary events lacking extreme emotional arousal (van der Kolk, 1994). Fragmentation of memory (Burgess, Hartmann, & Baker, 1995) and amnesia of the abuse or original traumatic event have also been reported in the literature (Briere & Conte, 1993; Williams, 1994). An innovative treatment approach capable of attending to these differences shows promise in the research literature, Eye Movement Desensitization and Reprocessing, EMDR (Shapiro, 1995). This approach uses rhythmic eye movements coupled with images or somatic memories of the traumatic experience, and strives to reduce the frequency and intensity of intrusive recollections from trauma.

Attending to the evolving standards of practice serves to enhance knowledge and clinical interventions. First, when using any new methods, therapists become educated, trained, and competent with the method prior to integrating it, e.g., hypnosis, guided imagery, or dream analysis. Informing the patient about the limitations and risks of the intervention and providing sufficient time for processing the material at the conclusion is important. When using hypnosis experienced therapists videotape or audiotape the session, after receiving written authorization from the patient, or prepare detailed written records of the events. Some states require such documentation for later criminal court proceedings specifically dealing with information discovered while under hypnosis. It is also important to be mindful of the types of questions asked and the phrasing used within the questions, so as not to lead the patient.

Therapeutic methods that are generally accepted by the mainstream professional community are preferred by psychologists who have been involved in the legal system. Limiting the use of controversial or experimental methods and obtaining informed consent for each method, explaining the risks and benefits becomes a sound practice. Presenting or recommending potentially controversial reading material to patients can also include information about the risks and benefits. Earlier editions of *Courage to Heal* (Bass & Davis, 1988) generated considerable controversy. This was partly due to its assumptions of childhood sexual abuse in persons who held suspicions of their sexual abuse and exhibited a constellation of specific symptoms. Recent editions include exploration of the memory debate and provide information on how to attenuate flashbacks and reduce dissociative states in the face of intrusive recollections. This inspiring self-help text is one example of the evolution of knowledge in the field of trauma and the benefits from constructive analysis, reflections from professionals in the field of child abuse, and feedback from survivors. It continues to be an important contribution to the self-help abuse literature.

When a patient begins to describe an abusive event, allow the information to be revealed at the patient's pace and in his or her own words. Using open ended questions is the suggested manner. Respecting and valuing the patient's timing is an overall critical issue in therapy with abuse survivors. This does not mean colluding with silence or avoidance of material, but respecting a patient's stated need or preference to proceed slowly. Sharing observations when a patient begins to stop speaking or dissociates from a memory when beginning to express it, can be highly supportive. This acknowledges the distress without challenging the patient to elaborate or go more deeply into the discomfort at that moment. This clinical practice "follows the psyche" by acknowledging the necessary and important defenses that have been built, without prematurely removing them. In fact, these adaptations may never be removed but may be slightly modified. I strongly believe in respecting the patient's timing and capacity to consolidate the progressively revealed information.

Therapists indirectly influence or bias the process of therapy or memory emergence based on beliefs about the pervasiveness of abuse or that abuse can be affirmatively assessed based on specific memories or behavioral cues. Multiple traumatic symptoms can result from a wide range of circumstances including sexual abuse and other types of interpersonal victimization such as rape or assault (Finkelhor, 1995). Legal advisors caution that therapists become vulnerable professionally when quick assumptions are made about the causal relationship between current symptoms and past events.

ELEVEN

Metal

Emergencies, Suicide, and Dangerousness

This chapter begins with the element Metal. The essence of metal provides structure, depth, and a conscientiousness to the work. Concentrated energy is often associated with metal providing discernment and clarity of thought (Eckert, 1996). These qualities are all helpful for work that requires awareness, the intellect, and application of wisdom in times of crises and emergencies. Crises can have both grave dangers associated with them as well as opportunities for immense growth, for both the therapist and patient. Two Chinese characters for the term crisis indicate both danger and opportunity. The complex symbolism suggests great potentialities for healing and transformation. The resolution of a crisis can yield to new behaviors, integrated ways of being, and a whole identity.

Crisis–Danger and Opportunity

The domain of psychological emergencies is categorized as medical and psychiatric. An emergency, the term derived from the concept of *urgenza* from the Italian literature, is perceived as an acute or intense situation, coupled with a serious or high level of danger, requiring immediate treatment or response. Examples are risk of suicide, risk of physical harm to others, states of seriously impaired judgment in which an individual is endangered-delirium, dementia, acute psychotic episode, severe dissociative state-and situations of risk to a highly vulnerable or defenseless person-abused child, dependent adult, or elder adult.

A psychological crisis, on the other hand, is a disruption of an individual's usual or *baseline* level of functioning, such that the usual coping responses prove inadequate. A crisis is often viewed as a loss of psychological equilibrium, the intrapersonal homeostasis is disrupted and the usual coping strategies become insufficient. Maladaptive coping responses may also be used. This distinction doesn't necessarily imply danger of serious physical harm or life-threatening danger, as in an emergency. Since many crises do involve psychological emergencies, it is important to distinguish between the two in the assessment process, and follow through with the appropriate level of intervention.

Crises involve substantial challenges to one's level of meaning in life, coping strategies, and support strategies (Aguilera, 1994). The nature of the subjective meaning that is drawn from an event will impact the potential development of the crisis. The lack of a support system can cause a moderately stressful event to plunge an individual into crisis. Crises can range from family issues and transitions such as divorce, acts of abuse or violence, alcohol intoxication, attempted suicide, and death, to adjustment to psychotropic medications as well as the development of neurological disorders stemming from head injuries or progressively deteriorating diseases such as Alzheimer's.

Crises call on the therapist to respond compassionately. One needs to assess the circumstances and implement suitable intervention strategies directed toward the patient's safety, although this may include the safety of others also. Responding to crises involves a reliance on the foundations of legal, ethical, medical, community resource, and clinical knowledge.

Crises may be situational or maturational. Situational crises involve unexpected events that are usually beyond the person's control, such as child abuse, natural disaster, sudden death of a loved one. Maturational crises occur during times of transition, for example when a child reaches adolescence, when a parent retires, and during other transitional periods, such as *mid-life* which Jung has addressed so eloquently.

Crisis Intervention Strategy

Approaching a crisis from the perspective of assessment, problem solving or treatment, planning, and termination frames the short-term nature of the work. Establishing rapport or a trusting connection is an important first step. A variety of methods can be used, including the expression of empathy, acknowledging and normalizing feelings, and supportively sharing one's own emotional response to the person or family in crisis. Next, one begins the assessment phase, where an exploration of the current problem or incident begins. Discussing the precipitant event through the use of open-ended questions yields substantial information including the individual's or family's prior level of functioning, coping methods, and identified strengths. Bringing in other sources of support that the family or individual desires is also helpful. Goals of crisis intervention are to assist in the alleviation of symptoms and prevent any psychological deterioration, thus allowing a return to a previous level of functioning, known as pre-morbid adaptive functioning. The planning phase can help the individual or family identify a specific issue to address one step at a time. Professional support can be provided in follow-up sessions and referrals for more intensive work can be given.

Safety is the primary consideration in crises. Assess the current safety of the individuals and maintain an unbiased attitude, avoiding words, gestures, and facial expressions that express or suggest shock and disapproval in potentially controversial situations. If you have the opportunity, clarify precipitating events to this crisis. Depending on the circumstances, a physician referral may be necessary.

Assist the victim and family members to clarify their thoughts and feelings through the process of stating responses and labeling feelings. Provide emotional support through encouragement and empathic listening. Convey concern and willingness to help alleviate stress. It is important to keep in mind that children may regress emotionally during times of stress or crisis, so it may be helpful to have a parent, friend, or trusted peer in close proximity.

Assist the family to mobilize their support network. Some social services programs such as in-home care may reduce environmental stressors that interfere with effective parenting.

Emergency Phone Call

When you receive an emergency phone call, your response is formulated with the intent to promote safety and stability and bring adjunctive help into play appropriately. Also protect confidentiality to the extent feasible. The welfare of the patient is essential.

Suggested Interventions:

1. Remain calm. Clinically assess the severity of the crisis the patient is experiencing, and the patient's ability to care for him or herself. Assist the patient in developing a number of options in the interest of insuring safety, such as asking a friend to stay over, mobilizing a personal support network, making an appointment for the next day. Contacting a law enforcement agency or mobile crisis response team could be helpful as well, particularly if the crisis is severe and the patient may wish to or need to be hospitalized. This may be the course of action you'll need to follow through on, depending on the situation.

2. Crisis intervention workers advise obtaining the phone number called from as soon as is practically possible. This permits the police to trace the call and respond to the scene to provide assistance and allows you to phone back if disconnected.

3. If someone other than the patient phones to provide information on a crisis your patient is experiencing, you

are required to protect the patient's confidentiality to the extent feasible. Your assessment of the information received, along with your clinical judgment of the case, and level of concern will dictate what type of action you take.

Defusings

Defusings were developed as interventions to use immediately after traumatic events (Mitchell & Everly, 1996). A defusing is a small group process initiated after any traumatic event or critical incident powerful enough to overwhelm the coping mechanisms of the persons exposed to it. The timing of this response differentiates it from a critical incident stress debriefing. It usually occurs as early as possible after the event, immediately if possible. The focus of the defusing is on small groups of people that usually work together, for example after a hostage crisis at a high school, one defusing may be engaged in with teachers, one with counselors, another with students in each respective classroom.

There are generally four goals to a defusing: moving toward a reduction of the intense reaction to the traumatic event; normalizing the experience so that everyone can return back to their work or duties; re-establishment of the social network; and assessment of the individuals involved to determine if a full critical incident stress debriefing is necessary.

Critical Incident Stress Debriefing

A critical incident is defined as any event with enough impact to produce significant emotional reactions in people immediately or at a later time. This is an event considered extremely unusual in the range of ordinary human experiences. The incident may be the foundation of the diagnosis of posttraumatic stress disorder if not resolved effectively in a timely manner.

A critical incident stress debriefing (CISD) is a group process employing methods of crisis intervention and educational processes, aimed at mitigating or resolving the psychological distress emerging from a critical incident or traumatic event (Mitchell & Everly, 1996). A debriefing is one element of Critical Incident Stress Management.

This type of group intervention can provide psycho-education and reassurance about the range of normal expected reactions to serious traumatic situations. It also gives clinicians the opportunity to suggest ways of coping with secondary stresses, traumatic reminders, and losses. As originally designed, a debriefing may take from two to three hours without a break, with one or two facilitators. The optimal time frame for a debriefing is from 24 to 72 hours after the critical incident. Debriefings are best held in functional workgroups also.

A primary goal of debriefing is to mitigate or alleviate the impact of the critical incident on those who were directly traumatized by the event. Debriefings are also appropriate for secondary victims, such as emergency services personnel who witnessed or managed the traumatic event, or tertiary victims, family and friends who may learn about the event from the primary victims.

A second goal is to accelerate the recovery processes in people who are experiencing normal stress reactions to these abnormal traumatic events. Additional objectives are to educate about the range of stressors, stress reactions, and provide information on methods of survival, allowing for an opportunity for emotional expression or ventilation. Mitchell and Everly (1996) reported participants benefit from reassurances that the stress responses are controllable and that recovery is likely. It is also helpful to foreshadow signs and symptoms which may emerge in the near future. A debriefing establishes a positive contact with mental health professionals, screens for people who need additional assessment or therapy, and provides referrals for counseling or other services.

Critical incident stress debriefing interventions have seven phases: introduction, fact, thought, reaction, symptoms, teaching, and re-entry. A brief summary of each phase is included. The introduction phase centers around introducing the facilitators, process, setting ground rules and expectations such as safety and confidentiality. The facilitators introduce themselves as the debriefing team and describe their intent, to work toward alleviating the impact of the traumatic event. Participants are asked to stay in the debriefing room. No cameras or recorders are permitted and the process is described as differing from psychotherapy and that the aim is to discuss the event in the presence of their peers. The step by step debriefing process is described, and the debriefers ask the participants to state who they are, what their role in the incident was, and what happened from their perspective. Each person is provided an opportunity to share.

**Seven Phases in Critical
Incident Stress Debriefing**

Introduction
Fact
Thought
Reaction
Symptoms
Teaching
Re-Entry

Fact Phase-CISD

The next step is the fact phase. Of all the elements of a critical incident, facts are often easier to initially discuss than attempting to talk about how one feels. The debriefing team asks questions about the participant roles or jobs during the incident and the events from their point of view. Emotions are not elaborated upon in this phase, but if emotions are expressed, they are acknowledged by the facilitators and the group is reassured that emotion is expected. The pacing is important so as not to emotionally overwhelm the participants in the early phase.

Thought Phase-CISD

The thought phase follows the fact phase. This phase begins with the facilitators asking the participants to state what their first or most prominent thought was once they were not longer functioning in an automatic mode. The thought phase serves as a transitional phase between the factual and emotional, between the cognitive and affective domain.

Reaction Phase-CISD

The next phase is the reaction phase, often the most emotionally powerful of the seven phases. The stimulating or trigger question centers on the worst thing about the incident for each individual. For example "What was the worst thing about this event for you personally," "What part of the event bothers you most," or "What elements of the situation cause you the most pain?"

Symptom Phase-CISD

The lengthy reaction phase is followed by the symptom phase, which moves the group back from the emotionally laden material into the cognitively oriented material. Participants are asked to describe any cognitive, physical, emotional or behavioral experiences they may have encountered while they were working at the scene of the incident (e.g., trembling hands, inability to make a decision, excessive silence or feelings of anger). Then the group talks about the various ways in which they experienced symptoms of distress while working at the scene.

Teaching Phase-CISD

After the symptoms phase, the group moves into the teaching phase, which naturally begins with a review or summary of the symptoms. The symptoms are normalized and described as commonly expected after the type of critical incident they experienced. This phase is cognitively designed in order to move the participants further away from the emotional intensity of the reaction phase. To close this phase, facilitators may ask what may given the participants some hope in the midst of their pain, or if there was something during the incident that made it less chaotic or painful.

Re-Entry Phase-CISD

The last phase of re-entry is an opportunity to clarify issues, answer questions, make summary statements and return the group to their normal functions. This phase brings closure to the discussions which have occurred during the debriefing. The debriefing team answers questions, reassures and informs as needed, states any feelings which are suspected to be present but were not mentioned, provides appropriate handouts, makes summary comments.

Dangerousness

Psychotherapists have a professional responsibility to protect other people from potentially dangerous patients and to protect patients from themselves. Therapists must know their responsibilities to warn and protect potential victims. The differential diagnosis process in evaluating dangerousness and violent behavior, includes evaluating for substance intoxication, schizophrenia and other psychoses, mood disorders such as bipolar disorder, impulse control disorder, antisocial personality disorder, and paranoid personality disorder. The following sections provide information relevant to patient dangerousness to self, others, and the therapist.

Patient Dangerous to Self

Bellah v. Greenson: A California Court of Appeals ruling that the Tarasoff mandated "duty to warn" did not apply to cases of threatened suicide. However, this case did establish a legal duty to take reasonable steps to prevent a threatened suicide. These steps depend on one's assessment of the level of danger, to prevent the threatened suicide. These steps can include measures such as a "no-suicide" contract, increasing the frequency of sessions, mobilizing the patient's support system, notifying a family member, and/or instituting involuntary hospitalization under the provisions of Welfare and Institutions Code § 5150. See Suicidal Ideation. Evidence Code 1024: "There is no privilege . . . if the psychotherapist has reasonable cause to believe that the patient is in such mental or emotional condition as to be dangerous to himself or to the person or property of another and that disclosure of the communication is necessary to prevent the threatened danger."

Suicidal Ideation

Responding to a patient's potential for suicide can be one of the more troubling and intimidating tasks faced by clinicians. A sensitive and comprehensive response is called for. Suicide occurs more frequently than homicide and continues to be a leading cause of death in America (Centers for Disease Control, 1997). Suicide also emerges as one of the leading causes of death for adolescents 10-19 years of age (Borowsky, Ireland, & Resnick, 2001). Becoming familiar with the risk factors is necessary for all clinicians. These risk factors include previous attempts, substance use, impulsivity, presence of lethal means, accessibility to firearms, hopelessness, depressive symptoms, psychopathology, financial hardship, physical illness, and lack of social support.

The potential loss of a patient can evoke immense concerns for the patient and patient's family in addition to serious concerns about the therapist's level of competence or continuation within the profession (Chemtob, Hamada, Bauer, Torigoe, & Kinney, 1988). Comprehensive clinical training in suicide prevention and risk management can provide adequate knowledge and experience to address these crises.

Suicide prevention approaches include action based methods (Bongar, 1992), systematic approaches to assess depression, suicide ideation, suicide plan, self-control, and suicide intent during intake interviews with suicidal patients (Sommers-Flanagan & Sommers-Flanagan, 1995), and integrated models combining affective and action-based interventions (Rosenberg, 1999). Additionally, *Dialectical Behavior Therapy* (Linehan, 1993) can be used as a treatment protocol to treat individuals with self harming tendencies and suicidal behavior who meet the criteria of borderline personality disorder. This approach synthesizes cognitive behavioral, feminist, and Zen theories with an emphasis on dialectics, the holding of simultaneous conflicting perspectives.

Suicidality is measured through a comprehensive clinical interview, review of ancillary information from previous outpatient and inpatient records, and psychological testing or use of assessment instruments such as questionnaires (Maris, Berman, Maltsberger, & Yufit, 1992). Beginning with a thorough clinical interview, suicidal risk can be measured on a continuum from mild, moderate, to severe. When suicidal ideation is present, a number of aspects can be systematically evaluated: the intent and motivation to die, precipitating factors, details of the plan, and the means being considered. Inquiries can be made of the suicidal thoughts, feelings, and the frequency, intensity, and duration of these.

The intent of suicide is a risk factor to consider. Having patients rate their intent from 0 to 10 can provide a sense of the imminence. "Intent can be rated as absent, low, moderate, or high" (Sommers-Flannagan & Sommers-Flannagan, 1995, p.45). When a plan has been made, the specific details, methods, and time frame being considered will be important. Inquiring about the means of suicide reveals the depth of contemplation the patient has given and provides more clues to the overall risk of suicide. If the patient considers a weapon, rope, or taking an overdose it is essential to know the accessibility of these.

Higher rates of completed suicide are correlated with intent and more lethal methods, including firearms, strangulation, and overdose. These are considered significant risk factors (Centers for Disease Control, 1997). The availability of firearms is correlated with suicide among children, e.g., Zwillich (1998) reported that guns figured in the suicides of 53% of children aged 1-14 years and 61% of children aged 15-18.

Suicide Risk Factors

Intent
Hopelessness
Physical Illness
Substance Use
Lack of Social Support
Accessibility to Firearms
History of Psychiatric Hospitalization
Depressive Symptoms
Financial Hardship
Previous Attempts
Impaired Thinking
Psychopathology
Lethal Means
Impulsivity

A history of previously attempted suicide is a significant risk factor (Olin & Keatinge, 1998) for suicide. Almost 80 percent of completed suicides were preceded by a prior attempt in a study by Schneidman (1975). Borowsky, Ireland, and Resnick (2001) found previous attempts to be the most important correlate in their longitudinal study of adolescents. Gay or lesbian orientation also emerged as a risk factor among 10-19 year olds, that cross cut gender and racial/ethnic groups.

Additional risk factors include the patient's sense of hopelessness, depressed mood, cognitive distortions, impaired thinking, impulsivity, intoxication, and judgment capacity. During times of depression, suicide risk increases when the mood shifts and the individual becomes anxious, agitated, or angry, indicating potential energy and increased motivation to carry out the suicide. Physical illness is also a contributing factor to risk, as is a history of psychiatric inpatient hospitalization (Olin & Keatinge, 1998; Pope & Vasquez, 1998).

Protective Factors or Deterrents to Suicide

Presence of Support Systems
Willingness to Access Support
Continued Employment
Financial Resources
Religious Values
Spiritual Belief

Protective factors or deterrents to suicide are equally important to consider when a patient is contemplating suicide. Significant deterrents involve the presence of support systems and the patient's willingness and capacity to seek these out. The presence of parent-family connectiveness was found to be an important protective factor for adolescents in Borowsky, Ireland, and Resnick's studies (2001). Threats to family cohesion may emerge during times of involvement in the legal system, disclosure of child abuse, and domestic violence incidents. Continued employment, financial resources, religious values, and spiritual beliefs also function as deterrents to suicide.

When a patient is imminently suicidal, providing safety and structure is essential. Safety measures may include the consideration of voluntary or involuntary hospitalization. When suicidal ideation is present but the risk is low, support systems can be mobilized, psychiatric or physician referrals can be made, and a number of clinical management measures can be taken. Noting the protective or life enhancing aspects of the patient's self such as the desire for help and a desire to live has been indicated as a helpful response (Rosenberg, 1999), as is working toward the elimination of the chosen means. Intensifying treatment by increasing the frequency of sessions, establishing a no-suicide contract, providing emergency or crisis line numbers, and addressing the underlying thoughts and feelings of suicide (Schneidman, 1992) such as emotional pain, despair, and hopelessness experienced by the patient (Rosenberg, 1999) are supportive measures. Longer range goals may center around the continued resolution of ongoing issues including the consequences of abuse, substance abuse, and depression.

Although there is no legal requirement to report, there is ethical responsibility to intervene. Therapists may need to break confidentiality by informing family, significant others, police, or psychiatric evaluation team. This is a situation in which confidentiality may be breached.

Initial Assessment

Suicidal Ideation
Intent
Plan
Means
Level of lethality

If there is ideation, assess the intent and the motivation to die, precipitating factors, ask about the details of the plan, and the means considered. Plan–inquire about the methods and the timeframe being considered; Means–inquire about what is being contemplated and how the means are available, e.g., weapon, rope, taking an overdose, jumping from bridge.

1) <u>If suicide is imminent</u>
   a) Work toward voluntary hospitalization,
   b) If patient refuses, initiate involuntary psychiatric hospitalization (Welfare and Institutions Code § 5150–72 hour psychiatric hold for evaluation and treatment) with police or other county designated personnel such as a Psychiatric Assessment Team, or Psychological Evaluation Mobile Team.
   c) Mobilize patient's support systems by notifying appropriate significant others.

2) <u>If suicide is non-imminent</u>–Suggested ways to manage suicidality:

a) Work toward eliminating the means, such as giving a weapon to law enforcement for safekeeping.

b) Increase frequency of sessions.

c) Have patient notify his or her support network, or assist the patient in doing so. If necessary, a containment by the support system could be initiated, such as a 24 hour watch.

d) Create a no-suicide contract with patient.

e) Establish daily call-in policy.

f) Give patient crisis or suicide hot line numbers and instructions on how to reach you in an emergency.

g) Psychiatric or physician referral needs to be considered. For example, if patient is on medication, refer back to psychiatrist for medication re-evaluation and consult with this professional (Schutz, 1982).

3) <u>Document in your records</u>: Ideation, intent, plan, means, previous attempts, your judgment about recurrent lethality; other relevant information including family history, alcohol or drug use, severity of depression, other precipitating stressors, actions taken, and results of actions.

4) <u>Long range</u>: Underlying difficulties such as substance abuse, depression, family history, chronic illness, and financial problems, will need to be focused upon for long range solution and problem solving.

Tarasoff Decision

When a patient communicates a serious threat of physical violence against a reasonably identifiable victim or victims, the therapist must operate as a *reasonably prudent practitioner* by making reasonable efforts to communicate the threat to the victim <u>and</u> to a law enforcement agency. "Psychotherapists who work with dangerous patients face a complex task of balancing the need of the patient for psychotherapy against the need of society for safety" (VandeCreek & Knapp, 1993, p.57). The therapist has an obligation to use reasonable care to protect the intended victim. This duty [to warn] is a required breach of confidentiality mandated by the *Tarasoff v. Regents of U.C.* court decision, and related legislation. Part of this duty might require warning individuals who could reasonably warn the intended victim. The preservation of life and safety is paramount within this decision. Related considerations include:

a) There is no *duty to warn* when the threat is made by someone other than the patient.

b) There is no *duty to warn* when there is no *reasonably identifiable* victim. For instance, when the patient describes a vague intention to go out and shoot a bunch of unspecified people. However, if the patient threatened to go into a specific store and shoot people randomly, the persons in the store would probably be considered identifiable victims.

c) If the patient is believed to be a danger to others due to a mental disorder, then involuntary hospitalization may be appropriate (Welfare & Institutions Code § 5150).

d) The psychotherapist is exposed to criminal and civil liability, when he or she fails to provide an adequate warning of violence to the victim and law enforcement authorities.

Serious Threat of Physical Violence: This is a phrase that is left open to interpretation, but it has been generally agreed that the term *serious* refers to the seriousness of the person's intentions rather than to the degree of violence threatened. Many have interpreted the term *serious* to mean *imminent*.

One important note here: This decision does not require psychotherapists to reveal a patient's idle thoughts or expressed fantasies of harming others. The court was quite specific in referring to the importance of breaching confidentiality when such a disclosure would prevent the danger to the intended victim or victims.

Because of the considerable impact on the patient resulting from the act of revealing confidential information to another party, this type of information is essential to share as part of obtaining informed consent to treatment, and/or to review when a patient is making these serious threats. A small but intriguing empirical study by Beck (1982) indicated positive effects (or no effects) were associated with prior disclosure and discussion of the necessity to breach confidentiality. However, when there was no discussion, a negative effect was experienced.

Dangerousness–Patient Dangerous to Others

When a patient communicates a serious threat of physical violence against a reasonably identifiable victim, the therapist must operate as a reasonably prudent practitioner by making reasonable efforts to communicate the threat to the potential victim, **and** to a law enforcement agency. The prevention of the violence may involve hospitalization of the patient, specifically when the severity of the violent ideation is extreme such as homicidal ideation, the patient's coping resources are minimal, and the presence of various factors, including the particular diagnosis and the capacity to maintain a no-violence contract.

Voluntary hospitalization would be considered prior to the more restrictive involuntary hospitalization. The Welfare and Institutions Code § 5150 allows for the involuntary confinement of a person, who as a result of a mental disorder is a danger to others, for 72 hour treatment and evaluation.

When engaging in therapy with a patient who may be dangerous, it is wise to use appropriate self-protection measures and structure. Provide a supportive environment that allows for the alleviation of symptoms through psychotherapy (perhaps increased frequency of sessions), social support, and medications. Psychiatric referral for a medication evaluation may also be appropriate.

With a rageful patient who may not be imminently dangerous to another, helpful goals are to provide for safety, structure, containment, and stability so patient will not harm self or others; to teach anger management and stress management techniques; to uncover and work toward resolution of underlying issues. In other words, to clinically address the issues which may diffuse the explosive situation.

Suggested Interventions
Rage and Dangerousness

Review Anger History
Teach Anger Management
Stress Management Techniques
Psycho-Educational Approach
No-Violence Contract

1) Review patient's history. Review how anger was handled in patient's family of origin. Note how the patient has dealt with anger in the past. Does the patient currently wish to deal differently with anger? Indicators of the potential for violence may include angry demeanor, substance intoxication, abuse, or use, poor impulse control, agitation, poor judgment, frustration, and irritable mood.

2) Focus on cognitions. Examine cognitive distortions or belief system, such as the use of mind reading; unrealistic exaggeration or expectations; irrational beliefs; investment in "shoulds."

3) Create a no-violence contract. Offer a no-violence contract to minimize the potential threat.

4) Utilize a structured approach with a focus on managing anger
   a) Teach a time out technique and distraction methods.
   b) Counting backwards from 100 or from 10
   c) Educating about the cycle of violence phases:
      1) Tension building,
      2) Acute episode or violent outburst,
      3) Loving respite or honeymoon phase, back to
      1) tension building, etc.
   d) Identifying anger triggers and avoiding them, or not responding to them
   e) Keeping anger journal or diary.

Dangerousness–Patient Dangerous to Therapist

Safety is an essential issue within psychotherapy, and the therapist's safety is integral in working with a patient who may be violent. If a patient is angry and irritable but not dangerous, the situation may be diffused by providing support or allowing for ventilation of feelings, in addition to setting limits on the parameters of behavior, i.e., acceptable vs. unacceptable behaviors.

Suggested Preventative Measures for Dangerousness

1. See patients when others are in office if danger is suspected–best not to see patient if you are alone in the office or building.
2. Have emergency phone numbers readily available.
3. Sit near the door, allow for patient's easy exit and never block the door.
4. Inquire about any weapons and request they be placed in the trunk of patient's vehicle.

Self-Protective Measures if Threatened

1. Inform others in your office or center, arranging for their support.
2. Leave the door to the office open.
3. Set clear limits on unacceptable behavior and describe the consequences of violent behavior.
4. If necessary excuse yourself and call for help (911).
5. Prepare for the possibility of defending yourself, i.e., disarming the person or fighting back.

Many county mental health departments or local agencies have courses in Managing Assaultive Behavior. These can be quite valuable in acquiring information on prevention and self protection including learning methods such as verbal interventions and paying attention to physical considerations.

TWELVE

Fire

Additional Forensic Matters

As we conclude, the Chinese character for the element of fire brings our work to a close. Fire is a powerful force representing an encompassing view of the myriad of issues related to the ethical practice of psychology. A new awareness that is "directed vertically upward, from deep in the earth up into the sky, from the material to the spiritual, from unawareness to consciousness" (Eckert, 1996, p.45). While previous chapters have focused on the intersection between legal issues and psychology, this chapter presents additional areas including essential parameters within psychotherapy and matters of interest to practitioners including child custody evaluations, grave disability, involuntary hospitalization, information on marriage and dissolution, mediation, subpoenas, and testimony. The chapter ends with reflections on social responsibility.

Child Custody Evaluations

Child custody evaluations are conducted when a suitable child custody arrangement cannot be agreed to by divorcing parents or parents who wish to restructure parental rights and responsibilities. The courts may modify custody and visitation rights until the children are 18 years of age. If you provide or provided psychotherapeutic services to a member of a family contemplating a child custody evaluation, it is considered inappropriate to function as an expert witness i.e., the child custody evaluator, for this particular family. However, it is likely that you would be interviewed or called to testify as a fact witness within this case regarding information you became aware of during the psychotherapeutic relationship.

Evidence code §730 indicates: "When it appears to the court, at any time before or during the trial of an action, that expert evidence is or may be required by the court or a party to the action, the court on its own motion or on motion of any party may appoint one or more experts to investigate, to render a report as may be ordered by the court, and to testify as an expert at the trial of the action relative to the fact or matter as to which the expert evidence is or may be required."

Qualified persons who conduct child custody evaluations include licensed marriage and family therapists, licensed clinical social workers, and psychologists. Psychological testing is often conducted and if the child custody evaluator is not qualified to administer and interpret the results, a referral to a qualified individual is made. Usually a minimum of a master's degree in a mental health field is required, with the additional training and knowledge of issues such as child development, divorce, and the legal standards and process involved in these matters. Competence to conduct an evaluation involves one's professional education, training, experience, and/or supervision.

When conducting an evaluation, the child's or children's best psychological interests are paramount. The evaluator is functioning as an expert witness, not as a psychotherapist or mediator. An expert witness is required to be neutral and non-discriminatory, focused on the parental capacity of each parent, and the psychological development and needs of the child. Data gathering techniques include history taking, clinical interviews with each parent and child separately and together, first hand observations in the office and home, psychological assessments, and ancillary information, such as pertinent knowledge from teachers, colleagues, relatives, and neighbors. If it is deemed appropriate and the child is mature enough, i.e., sufficient age and capacity to state a preference, the court will also consider the child's wishes.

An evaluation often results in a professional opinion containing a recommendation in the best interests of the child or children. Since the ultimate issue is actually decided by the judge, another way of understanding 730 evaluations, is that the expert witness assists the Superior Court Judge in making a decision as to the best custodial arrangement.

One last note regarding joint custody versus sole custody. In studies conducted by Ackerman and Ackerman (1997), experienced professionals indicated they preferred joint custody with primary placement with one parent or joint custody with shared placement. A less preferred child custody arrangement was reported to be sole custody with visitation privileges. Although a form of joint custody may be preferred, in high conflict or hostile and violent families, sole custody by one parent, with visitation privileges by the other may be the best possible arrangement. Many variables are weighed, including history of domestic violence, the amount of hostility, anger, and bitterness between the parents, willingness of the parents to enter into a joint custodial agreement, substance abuse, parenting skills and behaviors, move away issues, quality of the parent-child relationship, and psychological stability.

In terms of domestic violence during dissolution of marriage, Johnston and Campbell (1993) reported five basic types of interpersonal violence seen within custody disputes and the resulting impact on the children: ongoing or episodic male battering, female-initiated violence, male-controlling interactive violence, separation-engendered violence or postdivorce trauma, and psychotic and paranoid reactions. They recommended against sole or joint custody for a father who is involved in ongoing or episodic battering, and against sole or joint custody for a parent who is psychotic or has paranoid delusions. The safety of the children was of the utmost importance.

For more information on professional guidelines in conducting child custody evaluations, please refer to the American Psychological Association's Guidelines for Child Custody Evaluations in Divorce Proceedings (1994) and the Standards of Practice for Child Custody Evaluations promulgated by the Association of Family and Conciliation Courts (1995).

Grave Disability

Grave Disability is a term referring to a condition of being unable to care for oneself competently, due to a mental disorder. The patient is considered gravely disabled due to a mental disorder. When a patient is not competent to take reasonably good care of herself or himself, assessed in the areas of food, clothing, and shelter, a therapist may ethically breach confidentiality if reasonably providing for the health and welfare of the patient.

When a patient is believed to be a danger to others, or to himself or herself, or gravely disabled due to a mental disorder, the county may, upon probable cause, provide for an involuntary 72 hour hold for treatment and evaluation at an approved psychiatric health facility. This procedure may be invoked by a county designated person such as a member of a crisis team, a sheriff, a police officer, or a mental health professional. This procedure is authorized by California Welfare and Institutions Code Section 5150. Involuntary hospitalization may be necessary when a patient is gravely disabled due to some form of mental disorder and is imminently suicidal, out of control due to psychosis, etc.

Involuntary Hospitalization–W & I Code 5150

In California, when a patient is believed to be a danger to self or others, or gravely disabled due to a mental disorder, the county may, upon probable cause, provide for an involuntary 72 hour hold for treatment and evaluation at an approved psychiatric health facility. This procedure may be invoked by a county designated person such as a member of a crisis team, a sheriff, a police officer, or a mental health professional. This procedure is authorized by California Welfare and Institutions Code Section 5150.

A psychotherapist may become involved in initiating an involuntary hospitalization when the therapist has reasonable cause to believe that a patient meets any of the above stated criteria. Contacting the appropriate county designated professional, such as the Psychiatric Emergency Team, or Psychiatric Assessment Team, and explaining the situation, is an acceptable breach of patient-psychotherapist confidentiality.

Under the social policy of "deinstitutionalization" involuntary hospitalization, also known as confinement or commitment, is sought after less restrictive measures or alternatives have failed. The legal doctrine of using the least restrictive alternative requires that treatment be no more harsh, hazardous, or intrusive than necessary to achieve the therapeutic aims and to protect patients and others from physical harm. Sound clinical practice includes a first attempt to arrange for the patient to voluntarily hospitalize him or herself for appropriate psychiatric assessment and treatment, before seeking involuntary hospitalization.

Note: Only specifically county designated individuals may authorize an involuntary confinement. As mentioned above, treating psychotherapists may initiate involuntary confinements by requesting the services of a mobile Psychiatric Assessment Team or Psychiatric Emergency Team.

Marriage and Dissolution Laws

Laws regarding marriage and dissolution of marriage may provide valuable information for the practicing psychotherapist. For example, California is one of the states where common law marriage does not exist. Unfortunately, many unmarried couples mistakenly believe that if they reside in the same household for a minimum number of years (often 7) they have all the legal rights of a married couple. Additionally, minors experience an increase of rights once legally married, being treated as adults by psychotherapists. Legally, marriage is a civil contract between a man and woman who have each provided consent, "followed by the issuance of a marriage license and solemnization" (Family Code Section 300). This information is provided to round out some knowledge, however, if a patient requests legal information, a referral to an attorney for legal advice is essential.

Marriage and Minors. Minors wishing to marry are required to obtain written consent of a parent or legal guardian as well as a court order granting permission (as per Family Code Section 302a & 302b). However, premarital counseling is required.

Termination of Marriage. Dissolution of marriage replaced divorce as the legal term in the 1970's. Either spouse may initiate the dissolution on a no-fault basis, and the primary operable legal ground is a claim of irreconcilable differences. The other ground for dissolution of marriage is incurable insanity (Family Code Section 2312). The dissolution may be finalized as early as six months after the service of summons and petition.

Property Settlement. Community property assets (all property acquired during marriage, aside from gifts, inheritance, and separate proceeds of previously owned money or property), and community debts are divided equally, unless spouses agree otherwise.

Child Custody. The courts have jurisdiction to modify custody, visitation, and related legal rights of the parents at any time until the child is 18 years old. The guiding principle is that custody is determined in accordance with the best interests of the child. In order to determine this, a child custody evaluation may be ordered by the court (Superior Court, e.g., 730 Evaluation in California) or a required formal mediation process would be enlisted. Although the order of custody preference spelled out in Family Code Section 3040 begins with joint custody, in high conflict or violent parental relationships, joint custody is not recommended, since the continued violence, argumentativeness, and bitterness between the parents has been shown to be detrimental to the children.

Child Support. The decision concerning the amount paid by the parent(s) is based upon the need of the child, ability of the parent(s) to pay, and percentage of time spent with the child. A standardized computer program, Dissomaster, is currently employed in California. Rather than rely on the discretion of the court, the computer program creates the support figures based on the mother's and father's income, child care costs, other expenses, and the amount of time spent with the child. Either or both parents may be ordered to pay what is necessary for the support, maintenance, and education of the child. The amount is always subject to later modification until the child is 18 years old.

Spousal Support. The amount awarded to a spouse (formerly called alimony) is based upon need and ability to pay. Consideration is often given to the duration of the marriage and the employability of the spouse seeking support. The amount and terms may be modified by the Court at any time. Support is terminated upon death of their spouse, remarriage of the spouse receiving support, or other contingencies provided for in the settlement agreement or order.

Mediation

Mediation is a confidential process to assist divorcing or divorced parents work out an agreement about custody and visitation issues. A neutral setting is provided and the parents meet together and develop an agreement that is in the best interests of the child or children. A skilled and trained individual (often with a minimum of a Masters of Arts degree plus training and experience in conflict resolution) works as a mediator to assist the parents in this resolution process. The aim is to work out a parenting plan and set aside fault and blame. Many jurisdictions have mediation services connected to the Superior Court. California law requires that couples who disagree with the child custody or visitation orders must attend mediation before their court hearing on the matter.

When domestic violence is an issue, or a restraining order (protective order) is in effect, mediation can begin with separate interviews of the parents, and the parents can be escorted to and from their cars, or in and out of the court building by marshals. A parenting plan is created in these instances, in which the child's and victim's safety is assured. For further explorations of standards contact The Academy of Family Mediators (see Appendix).

Subpoena

A subpoena is an order of the court, which compels a witness to appear at a particular location, such as a courtroom, at a specified time, to provide testimony and/or records. The setting may be within a court hearing, administrative hearing, or a deposition. A psychotherapist may receive a *subpoena duces tecum*, which is a subpoena for documentary evidence consisting of records, notes, and billing information. These types of subpoenas cover notes in any form, including books, papers, audiotapes, videotapes, and computer generated information (Evidence Code § 250). When served with a subpoena, prudent action consists of claiming the privilege and contacting the patient and the patient's attorney regarding the best course of action (and document the course of action suggested). In highly complex situations, where the patient and attorney disagree on your release of confidential information or records, you should also consider seeking legal consultation, since failure to appear at the specified time and place could result in contempt proceedings.

Testimony

Psychologists may occasionally provide testimony within a court of law. Providing testimony can be a stressful or frightening experience for psychotherapists unfamiliar with this process. Psychotherapists can be called as either fact witnesses or expert witnesses, however expert witnesses are directly hired as such in civil or criminal matters, to provide specialized knowledge to the trier of fact (judge). A fact witness is a witness subpoenaed to testify to the facts of a particular case. A psychotherapist may be called as a fact witness through a subpoena. Brodsky (1998) offered the following maxim "explicitly relax or engage in productive work just before your court appearance" (p. 112).

Without an applicable legal or ethical exception, therapists never testify regarding a patient because everything disclosed by a patient to a therapist is considered confidential, including the therapist's thoughts based on such information (such as the diagnosis and assessment). This includes the fact that the patient is in therapy. The following exceptions are most relevant in the context of testifying in court.

There are basic exceptions provided by law, where the therapist may breach confidentiality and disclose information provided by the patient. Remember that it is advisable to seek out consultation or legal counsel when confronted with a complex disclosable incident or situation.

Disclosing Information in Court
Basic Exceptions Provided By Law:

1. Litigation exceptions:

   a. Patient's emotional condition is raised as an issue by patient or his or her legal representative;

   b. Litigation involving claimed breach of duty arising out of psychotherapist-patient relationship;

   c. *Breach of duty* suits by either patient or therapist: such as a malpractice claim or lawsuit against patient for nonpayment of previously agreed on fee.

2. Court appointed psychiatrist or psychologist: May testify if appointed at request of patient-defendant in criminal proceedings to determine whether or not to enter a plea of insanity.

3. Court or legally mandated disclosure: Some examples include reporting child, dependent adult, or elder abuse; or duty to warn about serious threat of bodily harm to a reasonably identifiable other.

Closing Remarks

Ethical decision making is critical to the overall functioning of a psychotherapist. Ethical conflicts often involve issues of autonomy, respect, right to privacy, confidentiality, self-determination, and the obligation to protect and promote the welfare of a patient. A significantly compelling aspect to ethical decision making is the expectation that the problem solving process be explicit enough to bear public scrutiny.

When faced with an ethical conflict or issue, an initial determination as to the parameters of the situation and the issues involved is essential, as well as a review of ethical guidelines and legal standards, coupled with a focus on consequences, benefits, and risks (psychological, social and economic) associated with an array of alternative decisions. An analysis involving critical evaluation and intuitive response can begin to clarify the situation. Further exploration with a colleague, consultant, supervisor, or attorney is recommended.

In summary, ethical behavior in clinical practice results from an ongoing integration of didactic information acquired through one's academic and clinical education, an awareness of and working knowledge of professionally relevant ethics codes and standards of practice, engaging an active problem solving methods, and personal traits and qualities of character, including maturity, awareness of limitations, knowledge of biases, responsibility, the capacity for informed judgment, compassion, and integrity. Hopefully, this review of issues has served a small role in supporting your continuing development as an ethical practitioner.

As the Tao is based in humanity, it is essential to end this work with a comment on social responsibility and action. I believe it is our obligation to respond and intervene in societal problems within our culture. One's unique background, societal interconnections, creativity, personal experience, culture, academic training, financial resources, felt sense of responsibility, and commitment will all determine the form of the response. It is my hope that scholars and practitioners of psychology will continue to think beyond the medical model rooted in curing disease and develop innovative and creative ways to transform social problems involving collective energy and vision.

Inspiration and motivation for social action projects can be drawn from religious and cultural communities. The Jewish tradition of Tikkum Olam which encourages a mission to repair the world is one example. In an article on the importance of instilling this desire in teens, Schwarz (1999) cited the importance of five critical principles that are integral to this effort: comprehensive societal information that instills moral outrage, empowerment that

FIVE CRITICAL PRINCIPLES FOR SOCIAL ACTION

1. Comprehensive Societal Information that Instills Moral Outrage

2. Empowerment That Channels Outrage into Constructive Engagement

3. Inspiration from Passionate Role Models or Mentors

4. Motivation that Comes from Deep Human Connectionwith Others

5. Contextualization

channels the moral outrage into constructive engagement, inspiration from passionate role models or mentors, motivation that comes from deep human connection with others who are different, oppressed, or marginalized, and contextualization whereby the social action is seen as a noble expression of the religion. Tikkum Olam provides a way to begin the process of creating solutions in society (Kline, 2000).

The Jesuit priest, academic psychologist, and revolutionary intellectual Ignacio Martin-Baro saw no political distinction between his religious and psychological work. He gave his life to the advance of dialogue and a liberation psychology (1994) that hosted a belief in personal and cultural transformation through the dialectical process of dialogue. He was assassinated along with seven others by Salvadoran security forces in 1989. His evolved vision of psychology was rooted in the core process of praxis, where the socially and personally constructed self is known through the world and through relations with others, an interdependent paradigm. Kovel (1996) referred to this consciousness as socially transformative. Through the consciousness of interdependence, liberation psychology provides a vision for effecting structural change within all dimensions of society. These potentialities instill a hope in a vision for a restored future. A future that hosts communities of involved, active, non-marginalized, and empowered members.

The practice of dynamic compassion known as *Ahimsa* is another way to effect change in the world and create the society that we desire. The way of dynamic harmlessness is a philosophy Mahatma Gandhi adopted, inspiring many to integrate or aspire to this spiritual approach to life. Ahimsa is a term having origins in Sanskrit and ancient roots in East Asian cultures including the Jaina, Hindu, and Buddhist traditions (Chapple, 1993). A practice dedicated to nonviolence, truth, the active expression of compassion, a deep understanding of personal responsibility, achieving peace through peace, and perceiving the ends and the means as "one and the same" (Altman, 1980, p.102). This active reverence for life can be expressed on many levels, and may be familiar as nonviolent personal action or respectful acts of civil disobedience. Ahimsa also inspires daily acts of compassion in thought, language, and relationship with others, situated within the larger community. This practice of compassion "necessitates a dialogical relationship between self and other, human and nature, human and animal" (Chapple, 1993, p.117).

Dialogical methods such as dialogue and council invite information from a variety of sources encouraging creative and collaborative learning. Dialogue is a process that allows for meaning to be shared and received by a group. Dialogue grew from Bohm's (1985) work in quantum phenomena as he searched for ways to effect cultural transformation. Bohm traced the roots of the term *dialogue* to the Greek *dia* and *logos* which means *through meaning*. Situating oneself in a group of people committed to dialogue is a frame for building community and collective meanings. Isaacs (1999) conceptualized dialogue as the profound process of thinking together and embracing different points of view. Ellinor and Gerard (1998) also expanded on this dialogue method bringing the process to varied business and work environments.

The methods of dialogue have empowered groups, created collaborative partnerships, inspired creativity and novel problem solving, and allowed for extremely difficult issues to be heard. Dialogue creates cultures of shared leadership and cooperation increasing partnership and inclusion. The fundamental values that form the deeply honoring perspectives within dialogue are the convictions that all members within a group have important contributions to make, a balance between inquiry and advocacy is held, the focus is on learning from others, and role or status is suspended. The intention of learning emphasizes understanding, relationships, the suspension of judgments, and making assumptions visible. This focus eliminates power over others, supports the discovery process, and synthesizes disparate points of view. Competition falls away and true community collaboration begins to develop.

The council process has also been a remarkably successful and authentic group method established in inner city schools, spiritual centers, and businesses, resulting in cooperative communities (Zimmerman & Coyle, 1996). Family councils have been created, in effect strengthening, invigorating, and building family connections through focused listening, speaking from the heart, lean expression, and spontaneous emotional sharing. The council process is engaged within a ceremonial environment akin to tribal circles and councils. A talking piece is chosen, representing the intentions of the council through its organizing symbolism. The talking piece is held by each individual who speaks, supporting the deep listening process. A shared silence may also be held during these times.

Perhaps as more psychologists, marriage and family therapists, and other mental health professionals become intimately familiar with the empowering and generative capacities of respect, honor, and inquisitive exploration through Taoist philosophy and methods such as dialogue and council process, these emergent cultures will synergize grass roots prevention and intervention efforts creating communities that children and adults thrive in. This kind of accessible and revolutionary vitalization embodies the potential to animate cultural transformation. A saying from the oral traditions of the Jewish Talmud exquisitely highlights our responsibilities as compassionate professionals: *It is not our responsibility to finish the work but we are not free to walk away from it.*

Appendix–Resources

Academy of Family Mediators.
  Non-profit educational membership association. Members provide mediation services to families facing decisions involving separation, marital dissolution, child custody, parenting, visitation, property division, wills and estates, elder care, spousal support, child support, pre-nuptial agreements. Annual conference, mediator referrals, and educational materials. 5 Militia Drive, Lexington, MA 02421. Phone (781) 674-2663. <www.mediators.org>

Adults Molested as Children United (AMAC).
  Referral source. Groups for all sexual abuse survivors; national referrals. PO Box 952, San Jose, CA 95108.
  <www.movingforward.org>

American Association of Marriage and Family Therapists.
  Professional association that provides approved supervisor designation. Located in Washington, DC, (202) 452-0109, New Code of Ethics effective July 1, 2001. <www.aamft.org>

American Association for Protecting Children.
  American Humane Association. National center promotes responsive child protection services in every community through program planning, training, education, and consultation. 63 Inverness Drive East, Englewood, CO 80112-5117. 1(800)227-4645.

American Association of Sex Educators, Counselors, and Therapists. A not-for-profit professional organization providing certification. Members include health professionals, clergy, researchers, students, and lawyers. Promotes understanding of human sexuality and healthy sexual behavior. Continuing education and conference. Box 238, Mount Vernon, IA 52314. Fax: (319) 895-6203. E-mail: aasect@worldnet.att.net <www.aasect.org>

American Counseling Association.
Professional association, not for profit, dedicated to the growth and enhancement of the counseling profession, provides grants to students, annual conference, code of ethics Alexandria, VA, (703) 823-9800. <www.counseling.org>

Americane Humane Association.
A non-profit association committed to the well-being of animals-provides materials on the connection between animal abuse and human violence. Englewood, CO. (800) 277-4645. <www.amerhumane.org>

American Medical Association.
Department of Mental Health. Provides referrals related to family violence and child abuse. Brochures on diagnosis, treatment, and medicolegal issues concerning child abuse. 515 State Street, Chicago, IL 60610. (312) 464-5066. <www.ama.org>

American Professional Society on the Abuse of Children (APSAC).
Organization for professionals in the field of child abuse treatment and prevention; offers advocacy, information, guidelines, referral services to professionals working in the field. Journal of Child Maltreatment. Oklahoma City, OK. <www.apsac.org>

American Psychological Association.
Professional association for psychologists. Many excellent journals of interest to mental health professionals, e.g., American Psychologist, Professional Psychology: Research and Practice, holds yearly conference, monthly newsletter: The APA Monitor. 750 First St., N.E., Washington, DC 20002. Phone: (202) 336-5500. <www.apa.org>

Amnesty International.
Campaigns to promote human rights worldwide, specifically those addressed within the Declaration of Human Rights. Recent campaign against the torture of children. <www.amnesty.org>

Board of Behavioral Sciences, California.
State licensing organization for marriage and family therapists, social workers, and educational psychologists. Responsible for consumer protection through the regulation of licensees, interns, associates, and corporations. 400 R Street, Suite 3150, Sacramento, CA 95814. (916) 445-4933. <www.bbs.ca.gov>

Board of Psychology, California.
State licensing organization for psychologists. Committed to protection of the health, safety, and welfare of consumers of psychological services.1422 Howe Avenue, Suite 22, Sacramento,

95825. (916) 263-2699. <www.dca.ca.gov/psych/>

California Association for Marriage and Family Therapists.
Professional association for marriage, family, and child therapists, representing over 25,000 members, including students, trainees, and interns. Monthly journal–The California Therapist. San Diego, CA 92111-1606. (619) 292-2638. <www.camft.org>

California Legal Codes.
Up to date information on the various California Codes relevant to the practice of psychotherapy may be viewed and downloaded on their website. <www.leginfo.ca.gov>

California Psychological Association.
Non-profit professional association for licensed psychologists and others affiliated with the delivery of psychological services. Special low-cost memberships for students. Yearly conference and monthly newsletter. 1022 "G" Street, Sacramento, CA 95814-0817. Phone: 916-325-9786 Fax: 916-325-9790. <www.calpsychlink.org>

Child Survivor of Traumatic Stress.
Electronic version of a newsletter for professionals who work with traumatized children. Articles include specialized assessments and scales for assessing post-traumatic responses. <www.ummed.edu/pub/k/kfletche/kidsurv.html>

Childhelp USA.
National Hot Line: (800) 422-4453. Offers a 24-hour crisis hot line, information, referral network for support groups and therapists, and reporting suspected abuse. Sponsors Adult Survivors of Child Abuse Anonymous meetings. c/o NSCAAP, PO Box 630, Hollywood, CA 90028. <www.childhelpusa.org>

Childwatch. Childwatch of North America.
National toll-free 24–hour information lines on missing children. (888) CHILDWATCH. <www.childwatch.org>

Childwatch International.
An international network for individuals and institutions conducting research on behalf of children. Special reports on urban childhood, child prostitution, and on-line access to a database on European Research. Headquarters in Oslo, Norway. <www.childwatch.uio.org>

Clearinghouse on Child Abuse and Neglect Information, National.
Provides annotated bibliographies of documents on specific aspects of child abuse or neglect, and provides statistics. PO Box 1182, Washington, DC 20012. (703) 385-7565. <www.calib.com/nccanch>

Defense for Children International, DCI.
A non-governmental organization founded during the International Year of the Child, 1979, dedicated to the legal and social defense of children internationally. Produces a kit of relevant international legal standards concerning the Rights of the Child. PO Box 88, 1211 Geneva 20, Switzerland. <http://child-abuse.com/childrens-rights/dci-what.htm>

Domestic Abuse Intervention Project (Duluth).
>A National information center. Provides information on domestic abuse including batterers' treatment information. (218) 722-2781.

Family Resource Coalition.
>Membership organization of social service agencies concerned with strengthening families through preventive services. Maintains a clearinghouse for information on family resource programs, quarterly newsletter. Chicago, IL (312) 341-0900. <www.frca.org>

Family Violence Prevention Fund.
>National non-profit organization that focuses on domestic violence education, prevention, and policy reform. <www.lgc.org/fund>

Feminist Therapy Institute.
>Promulgate the Ethical Guidelines for Feminist Therapists. Includes the integral significance of diversity and anti-racism. Feminist Therapy Institute, Inc., Corporate Office: 50 Steele Street, #850, Denver, CO 80209.

Incest Survivor Information Exchange (ISIE).
>Newsletter for survivors' writings, art work, & exchange of information. PO Box 3399, New Haven, CT 06515. (203) 389-5166.

Incest Survivors Resource Network International.
>Information and networking for survivors. PO Box 7375, Las Cruces, NM 88006-7375. (505) 521-4260. <www.zianet.com/ISRNI/>

International Critical Incident Stress Foundation, Inc.
>Educational organization providing national trainings for professionals. Critical Incident Stress Debriefing Model. 5018 Dorsey Hall Drive, Suite 104, Ellicot, MD 21042. (410) 750-9600. <www.icisf.org>

International Society for the Study of Dissociative Disorders.
>Educational organization; conferences, literature. 60 Revere Drive, Suite 500, Northbrook, IL 60062.(708) 966-4322. <www.issd.org>

International Society for Traumatic Stress Studies.
>Professional association. Journal of Traumatic Stress and monthly newsletter. 60 Revere Drive, Suite 500, Northbrook, IL 60062 (312) 644-0828. <www.istss.org>

National Board for Certified Counselors, Inc.
>Professional certification board which certifies counselors as having met standards for the general and specialty practice of professional counseling established by the Board. 3 Terrace Way, Suite D, Greensboro, NC 27403-3660. <www.nbcc.org>

National Center for Missing and Exploited Children.
>National clearinghouse and resource center. Funded by U.S. Department of Justice. Provides free single copies of useful publications. 2101 Wilson Blvd., Suite 550, Arlington, VA 22201. (703) 235-3900. <www.ncmec.org>

National Center for PTSD.
>Research conducted on posttraumatic stress disorder available on electronic databse. Provides a clinical quarterly on treatment of trauma survivors. <www.ncptsd.org>.

National Center for the Prosecution of Child Abuse.
American Prosecutors Research Institute. Legal clearinghouse, literature, research, and professional workshops. 1033 N. Fairfax St., Suite 200, Alexandria, VA 22314. (703) 739-0321. <www.ncjrs.org>

National Clearinghouse for Alcohol and Drug Information.
A communications service of the Center for Substance Abuse Prevention. Provides information on research, publications, prevention and education resources, and prevention programs, and a catalog. 11426 Rockville Pike, Suite 200, Rockville, MD 20852. (800) 729-6686. <www.health.org>

National Clearinghouse on Child Abuse and Neglect Information.
U.S. Department of Health and Human Services. For professionals seeking information on prevention, identification, and treatment of child abuse, neglect, and related welfare issues. P.O. Box 1182, Washington, DC 20012. (703) 385-7565.<www.calib.com/nccanch>

National Clearinghouse on Families and Youth (NCFY).
Tailors research to meet the needs of organizations, programs or communities; links people with others facing similar challenges in their work or who have creative ideas about improving youth practice and policy; provides updates on youth initiatives. P.O. Box 13505, Silver Spring, MD 20911-3505. (301) 608-8098. <www.ncfy.com>

National Coalition Against Domestic Violence.
National organization that works to end violence in the lives of families. Information, technical assistance, publications, newsletters, and resource materials. P.O. Box 18749, Denver, CO 80218. (303) 839-1852. <www.ncadv.org>

National Coalition Against Sexual Assault.
Advocacy, education, and public policy information. 125 N. Enola Drive, Enola, PA 17025. (717) 728-9764. <ncasa.org>

National Committee to Prevent Child Abuse.
Information and referral. Publishes educational materials that focus on parenting and child abuse prevention. Annual fifty state survey with statistics. Free catalog: (800)835-2671. 206 S. Michigan Ave, 17th Floor, Chicago, IL 60604-4357. (312) 663-3520.

National Organization on Male Sexual Victimization.
National organization devoted to research, activism, advocacy, and education. Publishes men's issues forum for male survivors. PO Box 380181, Denver, CO 80238-1181. (303) 320-4365. <www.malesurvivor.org>

National Organization for Victim Assistance.
Information, Referral, Community Crisis Response Assistance Training. Located in Washington, DC. (800) 879-6682. <www.try-nova.org>

Parents United International.
Dedicated to the assistance of children, parents, & adults molested as children, and others concerned with child sexual abuse & related problems. PO Box 952, San Jose, CA 95108-0952. (408) 453-

7616; Crisis line: (408) 279-8228. <www.giarretto.org>

People of Color Leadership Institute.

Goals are to improve cultural competence in child welfare systems that serve children and families of color. Institute has developed a cultural competence training guide and bibliography of publications about child welfare as it relates to people of color. 714 G St., SE, Washington, DC 20003. (202) 544-3144.

Sidran Traumatic Stress Foundation.

Non-profit organization dedicated to education, advocacy, and research to benefit individuals suffering from traumatic stress.Professional education and resources. Headquarterd in Maryland. <www.sidran.org>

Survivors of Incest Anonymous.

International network of self-help meetings, literature, pen pals, speakers, meeting information, and bi-monthly bulletin. SASE (two stamps) for information about support groups. World Service Office: PO Box 21817, Baltimore, MD 21222-6817. (410) 282-3400. <selfin.org/survivor/survorgs.1.html>

The Healing Woman.

Publishes monthly newsletter for women recovering from childhood sexual abuse. PO Box 3038, Moss Beach, CA 94038-3038. (415) 728-0339. <www.healingwoman.org>

VOICES in Action (Victims of Incest Can Emerge Survivors).

International organization for survivors and partners ("pro-survivors"). Conferences, special interest groups, & newsletter. PO Box 148309, Chicago, IL 60614. (773) 327-1500. (800) 7-VOICE-8 <www.voices-action.org>

REFERENCES

Academy of Family Mediators. (1988). *Standards of practice*. Lexigton, MA: Author.

Ackerman, M. J., & Ackerman, M. (1997). Custody evaluation practices: A survey of experienced professionals (revisited). *Professional Psychology Research and Practice, 28*(2), 137-145.

Ainsworth, M. (1989). Attachments beyond infancy. *American Psychologist, 44*, 709-716.

American Counseling Association. (1988). *Ethical standards*. Alexandria, VA: Author.

American Psychological Association. (1992). Ethical principles of psychologists and code of conduct. *American Psychologist, 47*, 1597-1611.

American Psychological Association. (1993). Record keeping guidelines. *American Psychologist, 48*, 984-986

American Psychological Association. (1994). Guidelines for child custody evaluations in divorce proceedings. *American Psychologist, 49*, 677-680.

American Psychological Association. (2001). *APA ethics code draft for comment.* Washington, DC: Author.

Arlin, P. (1990). Wisdom: The art of problem finding. In R. Sternberg (Ed.), Wisdom: Its nature, origins, and development (pp.230-243). New York: Cambridge University Press.

Arons, G., & Spiegel, R. (1995). Unexpected encounters: The wizard of Oz exposed. In M. Sussman (Ed.), *A perilous calling: The hazards of psychotherapy practice* (pp.125-138). New York: Wiley.

Association of Family and Conciliation Courts. (1995). *Model Standards of Practice for Child Custody Evaluations*. Madison, WI: Author.

Azar, S., & Siegel, B. (1990). Behavioral treatment of child abuse: A developmental perspective. *Behavior Modification, 14*, 279-300.

Bahm, A. (Trans.). (1958). *Ta Teh King*. New York: Ungar Publishing.

Baltes, P., & Smith, J. (1990). Toward a psychology of wisdom and its onto-genesis. In R. Sternberg (Ed.), *Wisdom: Its nature, origins, and development* (pp.87-120). New York: Cambridge University Press.

Bass, E., & Davis, L. (1988). *The courage to heal: A guide for women survivors of child sexual abuse*. New York: Harper & Row.

Baur, S. (1999). *The intimate hour: Love and sex in psychotherapy*. Boston: Houghton Mifflin.

Beck, A., Resnick, H., & Lettieri, D. (Eds.). (1986). *The prediction of suicide*. Bowie, MD: Charles Press.

Beck, J. (1982). When the patient threatens violence: An empirical study after Tarasoff. *Bulletin of the American Academy of Psychiatry and Law, 10*, pp.189-201.

Beebe, J. (1995). *Integrity in depth*. New York: Fromm International Publishing.

Berliner, L., & Conte, J. (1990). The process of victimization: The victim's perspective. *Child Abuse and Neglect, 14*, 29-40.

Berliner, L., & Loftus, E. (1992). Sexual abuse accusations: Desperately seeking reconciliation. *Journal of Interpersonal Victimization, 7*, 570-578.

Berman, J. (1990). The problems of overlapping relationships in the political community. In H. Lerman & N. Porter (Eds.), *Feminist ethics in psychotherapy* (pp. 106-110). New York: pringer.

Biaggio, M., & Greene, B. (1995). Overlapping/dual relationships. In E. J. Rave & C. C. Larsen (Eds.), *Ethical decision making in therapy: Feminist perspectives* (pp. 88-123). New York: Guilford.

Bohm D. (1985). *Unfolding meaning: A weekend with David Bohm*. London: Ark Paperbacks.

Bongar, B. (1991). *The suicidal patient*. Washington, DC: American Psychological Association.

Bowlby, J. (1980). *Attachment and loss: Loss* (Vol. 3). London: Hogarth.

Bradley, A., & Wood, J. (1996). How do children tell? The disclosure process in child sexual abuse. *Child Abuse and Neglect, 20*, 881-891.

Briere, J. (1989). *Therapy for adults molested as children: Beyond survival*. New York: Springer

Briere, J., & Conte, J. (1993). Self-reported amnesia for abuse in adults molested as children. *Journal of Traumatic Stress, 6*(1), 21-31.

Briggs, K., & Myers, I. (1976). *Myers-Briggs Type Indicator*. Palo Alto, CA: Consulting Psychologists Press

Brodsky, S. (1991). *Testifying in court: Guidelines and maxims for the expert witness*. Washington, DC: American Psychological Association.

Brown, L. (1991). Ethical issues in feminist therapy: Selected topics. *Psychology of Women Quarterly, 15*, 323-336.

Bugental, J. (1978). *Psychotherapy and process: The fundamentals of an existential-humanistic approach*. New York: McGraw Hill.

Bugental, J. (1990). *Intimate journeys: Stories from life changing therapy*. San Francisco: Jossey-Bass.

Burgess, A., Hartmann, C., & Baker, T. (1995). Memory representations of childhood sexual abuse. *Journal of Psychosocial Nursing, 33*(9), 9-16.

Burnett, B. (1993). The psychological abuse of latency age children: A survey. *Child Abuse and Neglect, 17*, 441-454.

California Department of Consumer Affairs. (1997). *Professional therapy never includes sex* (second edition). (One free copy available from DCA Publications, 401 S Street, Suite 100, 95814). <www.dca.ca.gov>

Caliso, J, & Milner, J. (1992). Childhood history of abuse and child abuse screening. *Child Abuse & Neglect, 16,* 647-659.

Canter, M., Bennett, B., Jones, S., & Nagy, T. (1994). *Ethics for psychologists: A commentary on the APA Ethics Code.* Washington, DC: American Psychological Association.

Cantwell, H. (1980). Child neglect. In C. Kempe & R. Helfer (Eds.), *The battered child* (pp.183-197). Chicago: University of Chicago Press.

Capra, F. (1988). *Uncommon wisdom: Conversatons with remarkable people.* New York: Bantam.

Casement, P. (1991). *Learning from the patient.* New York: Guilford.

Caudill, O.B., & Pope, K. (1995). *Law and mental health professionals: California.* Washington, DC: American Psychological Association.

Ceci, S., & Bruck, M. (1995). *Jeopardy in the court room: A scientific analysis of children's memory.* Washington, DC: American Psychological Association.

Centers for Disease Control. (1997). Regional variations in suicide risk: United States 1990-1994. *Morbidity and Mortality Weekly Report, 46*(34): 789-793.

Chan, W. (1963). *A source book in Chinese philosophy.* Princeton, NJ: Princeton University Press.

Chemtob, C., Hamada, R., Bauer, G., Torigoe, R., & Kinney, B. (1988). Patient suicide: Frequency and impact on psychologists. *Professional Psychology: Research and Practice, 19*(4), 416-420.

Children's Defense Fund. (1996).*The state of America's children yearbook.* Washington, DC: Author.

Conte, J., & Berliner, L. (1981). Sexual abuse of children: Implications for practice. *Social Casework: The Journal of Contemporary Social Work,* 601-606.

Conte, J., & Schuerman, J. (1987). Factors associated with an increased impact of child sexual abuse. *Child Abuse & Neglect, 11,* 201-211.

Crime and Violence Prevention Center. (2000). *Child abuse prevention handbook.* Sacramento, CA: California Attorney General.

Crittenden, P., & Ainsworth, M. (1989). Child maltreatment and attachment theory. In D. Cicchetti & V. Carlson (Eds.), *Child maltreatment: Theory and research on the causes and consequences of child abuse and neglect* (pp. 432-463). New York: Cambridge University Press.

Dass, R., & Gorman, P. (1985). *How can I help? Stories and reflections on service.* New York: Knopf.

Eckert, A. (1996). *Chinese medicine for beginners: Use the power of the five elements to heal body and soul.*Rocklin, CA: Prima.

Edinger, E. (1997). The vocation of depth psychotherapy. *Psychological Perspectives,* 35, 8-22.

Ellinor, L., & Gerard, G. (1998). *Dialogue: Rediscover the transforming power of conversation.* New York: Wiley.

Enns, C. (1996). Counselors and the backlash: "Rape hype" and "false-memory syndrome." *Journal of Counseling and Development,* 74(4), 358-375.

Enns, C., McNeilly, C., Corkery, J., & Gilbert, M. (1995). The debate about delayed memories of child sexual: A feminist perspective. *The Counseling Psychologist, 23*(2), 181-279.

Estes, C.P. (1992). *Women who run with the wolves: Myths and stories of the wild woman archetype.* New York: Ballantine.

Everson, M., Hunter, W., Runyan, D., Edelsohn, G., & Coulter, M. (1989). Maternal support following disclosure of incest. *American Journal of Orthopsychiatry, 59,* 197-207.

Factor, D., & Wolfe, D. (1990). Parental psychopathology and high-risk children. In R. Ammerman & M. Hersen (Eds.), *Children at risk: An evaluation of factors contributing to child abuse and neglect* (pp.171-198). New York: Plenum.

Faller, K. (Ed.). (1981). *Social work with abused and neglected chilren.* New York: Free Press.

Faller, K. (1989). The role relationship between victim and perpetrator as a predictor of characteristics of intrafamilial sexual abuse. *Child and Adolescent Social Work, 6,* 217-229.

Feminist Therapy Institute. (1987). *Feminist therapy code of ethics.* Denver, CO: Author.

Figley, C. (1995). *Compassion fatigue: Coping with secondary traumatic stress disorder in those who treat the traumatized.* Bristol, PA: Brunner/Mazel.

Fingarette, H. (1972). *Confucius–The secular as sacred.* New York: Harper and Row.

Finkelhor, D. (1995). The victimization of children: A developmental perspective. *American Journal of Orthopsychiatry, 65*(2), 177-193.

Freudenberger, H. (1974). Staff burnout. *Journal of Social Issues, 30,* 159-165.

Friedrich, W., Grambsch, P., Broughton, D., Kuiper, J., & Beilke, R. (1991). Normative sexual behavior in children. *Pediatrics, 88,* 456-464.

Fulton, D. (2000). Early recognition of Munchausen Syndrome by proxy. *Critical Care Nursing Quarterly, 23*(2), 35-42.

Gadamer, H.G. (1999). *Truth and method* (Second revised edition) (J. Weinsheimer & D. Marshall, Trans.). New York: Continuum. (Original work published 1960)

Garbarino, J. (1978). The elusive crime of emotional abuse. *Child Abuse and Neglect, 2,* 89-99.

Gates, K., & Speare, K. (1990). Overlapping relationships in rural communities. In H. Lerman & N. Porter (Eds.), *Feminist ethics in psychotherapy* (pp. 97-101). New York: Springer.

Gil, E., & Johnson, T. (1993). *Sexualized children: Assessment and treatment of sexualized children and children who molest.* Rockville, MD: Launch.

Gilligan, C. (1982). *In a different voice: Psychological theory and women's development.* Cambridge, MA: Harvard University.

Gottlieb, M. (1994). Ethical decision making, boundaries, and treatment effectiveness: A reprise. *Ethics and Behavior, 4,* 287-293.

Graham, A. (1978). *Later Mohist logic, ethics, and science.* London: Chinese University Press.

Greenberg, S., & Shuman, D. (1997). Irreconcilable conflict between therapeutic and forensic roles. *Professional Psychology: Research and Practice, 28*(1), 50-57.

Grudin, R. (1988). *Time and the art of living.* New York: Tickner and Fields.

Grudin, R. (1990). *The grace of great things.* New York: Ticknor and Fields.

Guggenbuhl-Craig, A. (1995). Foreword. In L. Ross & M. Roy (Eds.), *Cast the first stone.* Wilmette, IL: Chiron.

Guttheil, T., Gabbard, G. (1998). Misuses and misunderstandings of boundary theory in clinical and regulatory settings. *The American Journal of Psychiatry, 155*(3), 409-414.

Hall, J., & Hare-Mustin, R. (1983). Sanctions and the diversity of ethical complaints against psychologists. *American Psychologist, 38*, 714-729.

Hanna, F. (1993). The transpersonal consequences of Husserl's phenomenological method. *The Humanistic Psychologist, 21*, 41-57.

Hanna, F., Bemak, F., & Chung, R. (1999).Toward a new paradigm for multicultural counseling. *Journal of Counseling and Development, 77*(2), 125-134.

Hanna, F., Giordano, F., Dupuy, P., & Puhakka, K. (1995). Agency and transcendence: The experience of therapeutic change. *The Humanistic Psychologist, 23*, 139-160.

Hanna, F., & Ottens, A. (1995). The role of wisdom in psychotherapy. *Journal of Psychotherapy Integration, 5*, 195-219.

Hansen, C. (1990). *A Daoist theory of Chinese thought.* New York: Oxford University Press.

Hansen, C. (1991). Classical Chinese ethics. In P. Singer (Ed.), *A companion to ethics* (pp.69-81). Malden, MA: Blackwell.

Hart, S., & Brassard, M. (1991). Psychological maltreatment: Progress achieved. *Development and Psychopathology, 3*, 61-70.

Hart, S., & Brassard, M. (1994). *Draft guidelines for psychosocial evaluation of suspected psychological maltreatment in children and adolescents.* Chicago: American Professional Society on the Abuse of Children.

Hayden, M. (1996). When a lesbian client is attracted to her therapist: A lesbian therapist responds. *Women and Therapy, 19*, 7-13.

Hedges, L., Hilton, R., Hilton, V., & Caudill, O.B. (1999). *Therapists at risk– Perils of the intimacy of the therapeutic relationship.* Northvale, NJ: Jason Aronson.

Helfer, M., Kempe, R., & Krugman, R. (Eds.). (2000). *The battered child* (5th ed). Chicago: University of Chicago Press.

Hibbard, R., Ingersoll, G., & Orr, D. (1990). Behavior risk, emotional risk, and child abuse among adolescents in a nonclincial setting. *Pediatrics, 86*, 896-901.

Hill, M., Glaser, K., & Harden, J. (1995). A feminist model for ethical decision making. In E. Rave & C. Larsen (Eds.), *Ethical decision making in therapy: Feminist perspectives* (pp. 18-37). New York: Guilford.

Hillman, J. (1996). *The soul's code: In search of character and calling.* New York: Random House.

Hoffman-Plotkin, D., & Twentyman, C. (1984). A multimodal assessment of behavioral and cognitive deficits in abused and neglected preschoolers. *Child Development, 55*, 794-802.

Holroyd, J., & Brodsky, A. (1977). Psychologists' attitudes and practices regarding erotic and nonerotic physical contact with patients. *American Psychologist, 32*, 843-849.

Hopkins, B., & Anderson, B. (1985). *The counselor and the law* (2nd ed.). Alexandria, VA: American Association for Counseling and Development.

Hughes, L., & Corbo-Richert, B. (1999). Munchausen syndrome by proxy: Literature review and implications for critical care nurses. *Critical Care Nurse, 19*(3), 71-84.

Hunter, M, & Struve, J. (1998). *The ethical use of touch in psychotherapy.* Thousand Oaks, CA: Sage.

Irwin, L. (1995). The divine Sophia: Isis, Achamoth, and Ialdabaoth. *Alexandria, 3*, 51-82.

Isaacs, W. (1999). *Dialogue and the art of thinking together: A pioneering approach to communicating in business and life.* New York: Currency.

Jarof, L. (1993, November 29). Lies of the mind. *Time, 142*(23), 52-56, 59.

Johnston, J., & Campbell, L. (1993). Parent-child relationships in domestic violence families disputing custody. *Family and Conciliation Courts Review, 31*, 282-298.

Jordan, A., & Meara, N. (1990). Ethics and the professional practice of psychologists: The role of virtues and principles. *Professional Psychology: Research and Practice*, 21(2), 107-114.

Jung. C.G. (1954). Psychotherapy and a philosophy of life. In H. Read (Ed.) *The collected works* (R.F.C. Hull, Trans.) (Vol. 16). New Jersey: Princeton University Press. (Original work published 1943)

Jung, C.G. (1960). The structure and dynamics of the psyche. In H. Read (Ed.), *The collected works* (R.F.C. Hull, Trans.) (Vol. 8). Princeton, NJ: Princeton University Press.

Jung, C.G. (1971). Psychological types. In H. Read (Ed.) *The collected works* (R.F.C. Hull, Trans.) (Vol. 6). New Jersey: Princeton University Press.

Jung, C.G. (1973). *Letters, Volume 1, 1906-1950.* G. Adler (Ed.). Princeton, NJ: Princeton University.

Karcher, S. (1999). Crossed paths, crossed sticks, crossed fingers: Divination and the Classic of Change in the Shadow of the West. In C. Becker (Ed.), *Asian and Jungian views of ethics* (pp.9-42). Westport, CT: Greenwood Press.

Karcher, S. (1997). *How to use the I Ching.* Rockport, MA: Element.

Kaufman, J., & Zigler, E. (1987). Do abused children become abusive parents? *American Journal of Orthopsychiatry, 57*, 186-192.

Kavanaugh, K., Youngblade, L., Reid, J., & Fagot, B. (1988). Interactions between children and abusive versus control parents. *Journal of Clinical Child Psychology, 17*, 137-142.

Keith-Spiegel, P., & Koocher, G. (1985). *Ethics in psychology: professional standards and cases.* New York: Random House.

Kinnier, R. (1997). What does it mean to be psychologically healthy? In D. Capuzzi & D. Gross (Eds.), *Introduction to the counseling profession* (2nd ed.) (pp.48-63). Boston: Allyn & Bacon.

Kitchener, K. (1984). Intuition, critical evaluation and ethical principles: The foundation for ethical decisions in counseling psychology. *The Counseling Psychologist, 12*(3), 43-55.

Kleespies, P., Penk, W., & Forsyth, J. (1993). The stress of patient suicidal behavior during clinical training: Incidence, impact, and recovery. *Professional Psychology: Research and Practice, 24*(3), 293-303.

Kohlberg, L. (1981). *The philosophy of moral development.* San Francisco: Harper and Row.

Kohut. H. (1984). *How does analysis cure?* Chicago: University of Chicago.

Koocher, G., & Keith-Spiegel, P. (1998). *Ethics in psychology: Professional standards and cases* (2nd ed.). New York: Oxford University.

Laing, R.D. (1968). *The politics of experience.* New York: Ballantine.

Laing, R.D. (1982). *The voice of experience.* New York: Pantheon.

Lanktree, C., Briere, J., & Zaidi, J. (1991). Incidence and impact of sexual abuse in a child outpatient sample: The role of direct inquiry. *Child Abuse & Neglect*, *15*, 447-453.

Lawson, L, & Chaffin, M. (1992). False negatives in sexual abuse interviews. *Journal of Interpersonal Violence*, *7*, 532-542.

Leonard, L. (1989). *Witness to the fire: Creativity and the veil of addiction.* Boston: Shambhala.

Lerman, H., & Rigby, D. (1990). Boundary violations: Misuse of the power of the therapist. In H. Lerman & N. Porter (Eds.), *Feminist ethics in psychotherapy* (pp.51-59). New York: Springer.

Lipinski, B. (2001a). *Feng Shui wisdom.* San Buenaventura, CA: Pacific Meridian.

Lipinski, B. (2001b). Meridian Assessment Paradigm. In *Heed the call: Psychological perspectives on child abuse* (pp.139-144). Los Angeles, CA: Sojourner Press.

Loevinger, J. (1976). *Ego development.* San Francisco: Jossey-Bass.

Loftus, E., & Ketcham, K. (1994). *The myth of repressed memory: False memories and allegations of sexual abuse.* New York: St. Martin's.

Lorenz, H. (2000). The presence of absence: Mapping postcolonial spaces. In D. Slattery & L. Corbett (Eds.), *Depth psychology: Meditations in the field* (pp.225-243). Einsedeln: Daimon Verlag.

Loy, D. (1999). Loving the world as our own body: The non-dualist ethics of Taoism, Buddhism, and deep ecology. In C. Becker (Ed.), *Asian and Jungian views of ethics* (pp.85-111). Westport, CT: Greenwood.

MacIntyre, A. (1981). *After virtue: A study in moral theory.* Notre Dame, IN: University of Notre Dame Press.

Mair, V. (1990). Preface. In L. Tzu *Tao Te Ching: The classic book of integrity and the way* (V. Mair, Trans.). New York: Bantam.

Martin-Baro, I. (1994). *Writings for a liberation psychology.* Cambridge: Harvard University.

Marx, S. (1996). Victim recantation in child sexual abuse cases: The prosecutor's role in prevention. *Child Welfare*, *75*(3), 219-229.

Maslach, C. (1982). *The burnout: The cost of caring.* Englewood Cliffs, NJ: Prentice-Hall.

Milner, J. (1991). Physical child abuse perpetrator screening and evaluation. *Criminal Justice and Behavior*, *18*, 47-63.

Milner, J., & Chilamkurti, C. (1991). Physical child abuse perpetrator characteristics: A review of the literature. *Journal of Interpersonal Violence*, *6*, 345-366.

Mills, D. (1984). Ethics education and adjudication within psychology. *American Psychologist*, *39*(6), 669-675.

Milner, J. (1991). Physical child abuse perpetrator screening and evaluation. *Criminal Justice and Behavior*, *18*, 47-63.

Milner, J., & Chilamkurti, C. (1991). Physical child abuse perpetrator characteristics: A review of the literature. *Journal of Interpersonal Violence*, *6*, 345-366.

Moustakas, C. (1990). *Heuristic research: Design, methodology, and applications.* Newbury Park: Sage.

Myers, J. (1989). Expert testimony in child sexual abuse litigation. *Nebraska Law Review*, *68*, 32-34.

Myers, J. (1992). *Legal issues in child abuse and neglect.* Thousand Oaks, CA: Sage.

O'Hagan, K. (1993). *Emotional and psychological abuse of children.* Toronto: University of Toronto.

O'Neill, P. (1998). *Negotiating consent in psychotherapy.* New York: New York University Press.

Office of the Attorney General. (June 28, 1984). *Opinion of John K. Van De Kamp, Attorney General. No. 83-810.* Sacramento, CA: Office of the Attorney General.

Olin, J., & Keatinge, C. (1998). *Rapid psychological assessment.* New York: John Wiley.

Oxford dictionary of English etymology. (1966). New York: Oxford University Press.

Pearlman, L., & Saakvitne, K. (1995). The therapeutic relationship as the context for countertransference and vicarious traumatization. In *Trauma and the therapist* (pp.15-34). New York: W. W. Norton.

Pesut, D. (1990). Creative thinking as a self-regulatory metacognitive process: A model for education, traninig, and further research. *Journal of Creative Behavior, 24,* 105-110.

Polansky, N., Chalmers, M., Buttenwieser, E., & Williams, D. (1991). *Damaged parents: An anatomy of child neglect.* Chicago: University of Chicago Press.

Pope, K. (1991). Dual relationships in psychotherapy. *Ethics and Behavior, 1,* 21-34.

Pope, K. (1996). Scientific research, recovered memory, and context: Seven surprising findings. *Women and Therapy, 19,* 123-140.

Pope, K., & Bajt, T. (1988). When laws and values conflict: A dilemma for psychologists. *American Psychologist, 43,* 828.

Pope, K., & Bouhoutsos, J. (1986). *Sexual intimacy between therapists and patients.* New York: Praeger.

Pope, K., & Brown, L. (1996). *Recovered memories of abuse: Assessment, therapy, forensics.* Washington, DC: American Psychological Association.

Pope, K., & Caudill, O.B. (2000). The impact of recovered memories. In F. Kaslow (Ed.), *Handbook of couple and family forensics: A sourcebook for mental health and legal professionals* (pp.375-399). New York: John Wiley.

Pope, K., Keith-Speigel, P., & Tabachnick, B. (1986). Sexual attraction to clients: The human therapist and the (sometimes) inhuman training system. *American Psychologist, 41,* 147-158.

Pope, K., Tabachnick, B., & Keith-Spiegel, P. (1987). Ethics of practice: The beliefs and behaviors of psychologists as therapists. *American Psychologist, 42,* 993-1006.

Pope, K., & Vasquez, M. (1991). *Ethics in psychotherapy and counseling: A practical guide for psychologists.* San Francisco: Jossey-Bass.

Pope, K., & Vasquez, M. (1998). *Ethics in psychotherapy and counseling: A practical guide.* San Francisco: Jossey-Bass.

Porter, N. (1995). Therapist self-care: A proactive ethical approach. In H. Lerman & N. Porter (Eds.), *Feminist ethics in psychotherapy* (pp.247-266). New York: Springer.

Ricoeur, P. (1978). Hermeneutics. In C. Regan & D. Stewart (Eds.), *The philosophy of Paul Ricoeur.* Boston: Beacon.

Rieser, M. (1991). Recantation in child sexual abuse cases. *Child Welfare, 70,* 611-621.

The Tao of Integrity–REFERENCES

Rilke, R.M. (1984). *Letters to a young poet.* (S. Mitchell, Trans.). New York: Random House.

Rohner, R., & Rohner, E. (1980). Antecedents and consequences of parental rejection: A theory of emotional abuse. *Child Abuse & Neglect, 4,* 189-198.

Rosenberg, J. (1999). Suicide prevention: An integrated training model using affective and action-based interventions. *Professional Psychology: Research and Practice, 30*(1), 83--87.

Rychlak, J. (Ed.). (1976). *Dialectic: Humanistic rationale for behavior and development.* New York: S. Karger.

Safran, C. (1993). Dangerous obsession: The truth about repressed memories. *McCall's,* pp.98, 102, 105, 106, 108, 109, & 155.

Salgo v. Stanford University. (1957). 317 P2d 170 (California Court of Appeal).

Samuels, A. (1989). *The plural psyche.* London: Routledge.Schneidman, E. (1975). *Suicidology: Contemporary developments.* New York: Grune & Stratton.

Sardello, R. (1988). The illusion of infection: A cultural psychology of AIDS. *Spring,* 15-26.

Sauzier, M. (1989). Disclosure of sexual abuse. *Pediatric Clinics of North America, 12,* 445-471.

Schamess, G. (1999). Therapeutic love and its permutations. *Clinical Social Work Journal, 27,* 9-26.

Schutz, B. (1982). *Legal liability to psychotherapy.* San Francisco: Jossey-Bass.

Schwartz-Salant, N. (1984). Archetypal factors underlying sexual acting-out in the transference/countertransference process. In N. Schwartz & M. Stein (Eds.), *Transference countertransference* (pp.1-30). Wilmette, IL: Chiron.

Sears, V. (1990). On being an "only" one. In H. Lerman & N. Porter (Eds.), *Feminist ethics in psychotherapy* (pp.102-105). New York: Springer.

Sexton, T., & Whiston, S. (1991). A review of the empirical basis for counseling: Implications for practice and training. *Counselor Education and Supervision, 30,* 330-354.

Sgroi, S. (1982). *Handbook of clinical intervention in child sexual abuse.* Lexington, MA: Lexington.

Shapiro, F. (1995). *Eye movement desensitization and reprocessing: Basic principles, protocols, and procedures.* New York: Guilford.

Shengold, L. (1979). Child abuse and deprivation: Soul murder. *Journal of the American Psychoanalytic Association, 27,* 533-599.

Shengold, L. (1989). *Soul murder: The effects of childhood abuse and deprivation.* New York: Fawcett Columbine.

Singer, J. (1994). *Boundaries of the soul: The practice of Jung's psychology.* New York: Doubleday.

Singer, M., Petchers, M., & Hussey, D. (1989). The relationship between sexual abuse and substance abuse among psychiatrically hospitalized adolescents. *Child Abuse & Neglect, 13,* 319-325.

Skolimowski, H. (1994). *The participatory mind: A new theory of knowledge and of the universe.* New York: Penguin.

Skorupa, J., & Agresti, A. (1993). Ethical beliefs about burnout and continued professional practice. *Professional Psychology: Research and Practice, 24*(3), 281-285.

Smith, A. (1990). Working within the lesbian community: The dilemma of overlapping relationships. In H. Lerman & N. Porter (Eds.), *Feminist ethics in psychotherapy* (pp.92-96). New York: Springer.

Sommers-Flanagan, J., & Sommers-Flanagan, R. (1995). Intake interviewing with suicidal patients: A systematic approach. *Professional Psychology: Research and Practice, 26*(1), 41-47.

Sorenson, T., & Snow, B. (1991). How children tell: The process of disclosure in child sexual abuse. *Child Welfare, 70*, 3-15.

Stebnicki, M. (2000). Stress and grief reactions among rehabilitation professionals: Dealing effectively with empathy fatigue. *Journal of Rehabilitation, 66*(1), 23-29.

Sternberg, R. (1986). Intelligence, wisdom, and creativity: Three is better than one. *Educational Psychologist, 21*, 175-190.

Sternberg, R. (1990). Wisdom and its relations to intelligence and creativity. In R. Sternberg (Ed.), *Wisdom: Its nature, origins, and development* (pp.142-159). New York: Cambridge University Press.

Summit, R. (1983). The child sexual abuse accommodation syndrome. *Child Abuse and Neglect, 7*, 177-193.

Tarasoff v. Board of Regents of the University of California, Cal. Rptr. 14, No. S.F. 23042 (Cal. Sup. Ct., July 1, 1976) 131.

Taylor, D. (1997). *Disappearing acts.* Durham: Duke University.

Tolman, C. (1983). Further comments on the meaning of "dialectic." *Human Development, 26*, 320-324.

Trickett, P., & Kuczynski, L. (1986). Children's misbehaviors and parental discipline strategies in abusive and nonabusive families. *Developmental Psychology, 27*, 148-158.

Tymchuk, A. (1986). Guidelines for ethical decision making. *Canadian Psychology, 27*, 36-43.

Urquiza, A., & Keating, L. (1990). The prevalence of sexual abuse of males. In M. Hunter (Ed.), *The sexually abused male, Vol. 1: Prevalence, impact, and treatment* (pp.90-103). Lexington, MA: Lexington Books.

van der Kolk, B. (1994). The body keeps the socre: Memory and the evolving psychobiology of posttraumatic stress. *Harvard Review of Psychiatry, 1*(5), 253-265.

van der Kolk, B., Blitz, R., Burr, W., & Hartmann, E. (1984). Nightmares and trauma: Lifelong and traumatic nightmares in Veterans. *American Journal of Psychiatry, 141*, 187-190.

van der Kolk, B., Perry, J., & Herman, J. (1991). Childhood origins of self-destructive behavior. *American Journal of Psychiatry, 148*, 1665-1671.

VandeCreek, L., & Knapp, S. (1993). *Tarasoff and beyond: Legal and clinical considerations in the treatment of life-endangering patients.* Sarasota, FL: Professional Resource Press.

von Franz, M.L. (1980). *Alchemy: An introduction to the symbolism and the psychology.* Toronto, Canada: Inner City Books.

Walker, B. (1986). The I Ching of the goddess. San Francisco: HarperCollins.

Watkins, B., & Bentovim, A. (1992). The sexual abuse of male children and adolescents: A review of current research. *Journal of Child Psychology and Psychiatry and Allied Disciplines, 33*(1), 197-248.

Watts, A. (1975). *Psychotherapy East and West.* New York:Basic.

Webster's II New Riverside University Dictionary. (1984). Boston, MA: Houghton Mifflin.

Weissbourd, R. (1996). *The vulnerable child*. Reading, MA: Addison-Wesley.

Welfel, E. (1998). *Ethics in counseling and psychotherapy: Standards, research, and emerging issues*. Pacific Grove, CA: Brooks/Cole.

Whitmont, E. (1978). *The symbolic quest: Basic concepts of analytical psychology*. Princeton, NJ: Princeton University Press.

Widom, C. (1989). Does violence beget violence? A critical examination of the literature. *Psychological Bulletin, 106*, 3-28.

Wilhelm, R. (1977). *Heaven, earth, and man in the Book of Changes*. Seattle, WA: University of Washington Press.

Williams, L. (1994). Adult memories of childhood abuse. *Journal of Consulting and Clinical Psychology, 62*(6), 1167-1176.

Wylie, M. (1993). Trauma and memory. *The Family Therapy Networker, 17*(5), 42-43.

Zimmerman, J., & Coyle, V. (1996). *The way of council*. Las Vegas, NV: Bramble Books.

Zwillich, T. (1998). Risk factors for suicide in children. *Clinical Psychiatry News, 26*(6):18.

INDEX

A

abandonment 139, 163, 166, 167, 191
abdominal injuries 188
Academy of Family Mediators
    233, 241, 247
Ackerman 227, 247
acute episode 184
adult abuse 162–167
advertising 30, 54, 104–106
Adults Molested as Children United 241
advocacy 238, 242, 245, 247
Ahimsa 237, 238
AIDS 48, 132
Ainsworth 186, 191, 249
ambiguity 24, 29, 51, 55
American Association for Protecting
    Children 241
American Association of Marriage and
    Family Therapy 241
American Association of Sex Educators,
    Counselors, 242
American Counseling Association
    242, 247
American Medical Association 242
American Professional Society on the Abuse
    of Chil 242
American Psychological Association
    74, 79, 228, 242, 247, 248, 249,
    254
ancient traditions 15

Anderson 55, 251

anger 164, 210, 211, 218, 219, 220, 221,
    222, 228, 229, 256
anxiety 39, 55, 86, 151, 194, 195;
                anxiety management 151
archetypal 78, 99
Arons 75, 247
aspirational 27, 31, 50, 92, 104

assessment
    60, 64, 65, 66, 70, 78, 90, 96,
    105, 110, 120, 128, 129, 148, 149,
    150, 154, 155, 156, 157, 167, 168,
    203, 204, 206, 207, 211, 227, 229,
    230, 234;
    initial assessment 216;
        of suicide 227-229

Association of Family and Conciliation
    Courts 228, 247

attachment 35, 79, 187, 190, 193

attributions 183
authentic meetings 25
autonomy 34, 44, 45
awareness 16, 19, 23, 25, 37, 38, 39, 47
Azar 183, 247

B

Bagua 18, 19

259

Biographical Sketch

Dr. Barbara Lipinski is a licensed psychologist and family and child therapist in Southern California. Prior to her work as a police psychologist with the Los Angeles Police Department in 2000, she was a member of the core faculty at Pacifica Graduate Institute for ten years. She held positions as the Clinical Coordinator of the Counseling Psychology Program, the Research Coordinator of the Overseas Program, and Chair of the Counseling Psychology Program-Ladera campus. She has devoted her practice to working with psychotherapists, victims of violent crime, and law enforcement professionals.

She received her doctorate at the University of Southern California and holds clinical membership with the American Psychological Association, California Association of Marriage and Family Therapists, California Psychological Association, American Professional Society on the Abuse of Children, Psychologists for the Ethical Treatment of Animals, and is an Associate Member of the International Association of Chiefs of Police. Her lifetime community college instructor credential is in psychology, public services, and administration.

She serves as a forensic witness for the California Board of Behavioral Sciences and is a Diplomate of the American Board of Forensic Examiners, Life Fellow of the American College of Forensic Examiners. She is currently the co-chair of the Ethics Committee and CLASP for the Ventura County Psychological Association.